D1341744

IN THE WAKE
OF THE
VITAL SPARK

In the Wake of the Vital Spark

Para Handy's Scotland

STUART DONALD

Johnston & Bacon
Stirling

First published in Great Britain in 1994 by
Johnston & Bacon Books Limited
PO Box No 1
Stirling FK7 0BH

ISBN   0 7179 4604 5 (Hardcover)
       0 7179 4605 3 (Paperback)

Printed in Great Britain

Contents

West Coast
of Scotland

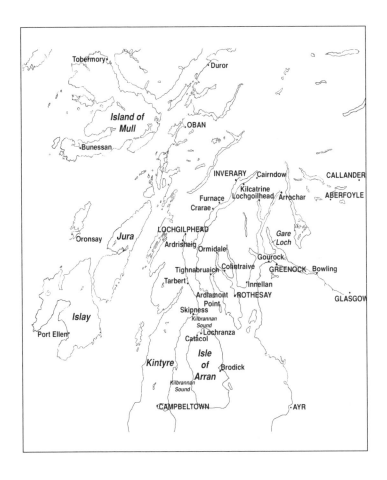

Acknowledgements

This book could never have been written without the benefit of the advice and shared experience which was so generously given me by folk who not only echoed my own enthusiasm for the magic world which Neil Munro created, but had a first-hand experience of its real-life equivalent.

To Ian McColl, erstwhile owner of the three-handed estuary puffer **Craigielea;** his nephew Duncan, who crewed on the five-man boats of Ross & Marshall in the '50s; George Anderson, who was Ross & Marshall's Marine Superintendent from 1956 till 1970 – my sincerest thanks. Apart from their knowledge of a lost way of life, the most remarkable thing about them all is the affection with which they look back on experiences which at the time were always demanding, often uncomfortable, and sometimes downright dangerous.

Eoin McArthur not only had sailed on puffers but was able to shed new light on the identity of the "real" Para Handy: and provide evidence which reinforced my own theories about the new stories in the Birlinn edition – in both instances drawing on his family's friendship and kinship with Neil Munro himself.

Bill Scott, Local Studies Librarian with Argyll and Bute District Council, Dunoon, helped substantially in tracking down background material, and suggesting valuable new sources for information and investigation.For the turn-of-the-century black and white photographs I am indebted to District Librarian Andrew Ewan for giving me access to the remarkable Macgrory collection in the archives of the Argyll and Bute District Libraries. My thanks go to Bookpoint, Dunoon for the print of Norman Whitla's beached puffer used on the cover and to Paul McKay, Bute for the frontispiece photograph of the **Vital Spark** at Kilchattan Bay.

There can be no better proof of the universal and undiminished appeal of the puffers than that I received letters from Donald Clarke, formerly of Greenock but now living in South Africa, who had heard about my projected book, and took the trouble to write to tell me of his days on the puffer **Mellite** in the 1930s. My thanks to him, and to everyone else who encouraged me to set down on paper something of the lost world of Para Handy.

Finally, a special tribute to a man who has proved that that world is still not *totally* lost. While the converted puffers **VIC 32** and **Auld Reekie** perform sterling service in carrying tourists on mini-cruises in the waters of the west, the ship-owner Chris Nicholson is providing, in the 1990s, exactly the same type of cargo service to the remote communities as Para Handy was offering in the 1890s – with the very last of the true, working puffers: **Eilean Eisdeal**, formerly **VIC 72**, built in Hull in 1944 and still carrying kit-houses to Coll and coals to Castlebay.

Introduction

In the ninety years or so since the exploits of the **Vital Spark** and her captain first appeared in print in the pages of the *Glasgow Evening News,* the puffer and her crew have become a national institution – and not only in Scotland. This present volume is intended to be a general companion and guide to the real turn-of-the-century Clyde from which Neil Munro drew his inspiration – and to the imaginary world which he created and peopled with such timeless characters. It is hoped that it will give some pleasure even to those who are as fond of and familiar with the Para Handy stories as the author is: and that it will encourage anyone who has not yet read the originals to do so without delay. It is ironic that, as most Para Handy fans know, Neil Munro himself prized the stories but little. As well as being a working journalist – which is how these stories came to be written, for his regular columns in the *Evening News* – he was also a serious and, earlier this century at least, a reputed novelist. His historical novels, mostly set in and around the Highlands he knew so well, were what he saw as his life's work. The Para Handy stories he only allowed to be published under the alias of 'Hugh Foulis'.

Today, his novels – *Doom Castle, The New Road, The Shoes of Fortune* and the rest – tend to gather dust on forgotten shelves. But Para Handy's popularity has never been greater. In 1991 a brand new edition was brought out by the Birlinn Press, which included 18 stories never before published in book form. A new series has been produced for BBC television, with Gregor Fisher in the role of the skipper made famous two decades ago by Roddy MacMillan, and before *that* by Duncan Macrae. There can be no greater tribute to Neil Munro's enduring and endearing qualities as a gifted observer and chronicler of his world than the perennial popularity of the tales which, in his own lifetime, he dismissed as "slight".This is not to diminish the style with which his serious writing was created. But many authors have written novels similar to and just as good as the Neil Munro 'romances'.

Yet nobody, in this country or any other, has ever managed to create a cast of characters, or a series of episodes, which so perfectly capture a long-lost age. No other writer has been able to pen stories that are as funny and as fresh today as they were when written ninety years ago. Neil Munro's supreme talent was to observe – and to set down on paper tales marked by a gentle humour, inspired by the people he met and the things he saw, which instantly entertain those new to them and, perhaps the sternest test of all, are still irresistibly funny to those re-reading, for the umpteenth time, stories which they virtually know by heart. The writing for which he is world-famous today may not be that for which he expected, or indeed wished, to be remembered. But the stories which he dismissed as ephemeral have proved to be the lasting monument to his unique talent.They have cheered and brightened the lives of everyone who has read them. Neil Munro could ask for no finer epitaph or more fitting tribute than the genuine and lasting affection in which countless readers worldwide hold him – in gratitude for the tales and the characters which he created for their entertainment.

Para Handy's
Real World

CHAPTER 1
Some Ports and Harbours

The communities in and around the Clyde Estuary and many of its adjacent islands were the backdrop against which Neil Munro staged the fictional exploits of the **Vital Spark** and her crew. Given the authenticity of that setting, a brief account of the character of some of these communities at the close of the Victorian age is the logical starting point for a journey through the real world of Para Handy. The chapters which follow will look first at the more general traffic and way of life on the river, and then at the puffers and the men who crewed them, in Para Handy's time and in the decades which followed. The lifestyle of the puffer crews was little changed over two generations.

The introductory cliché would be to suggest that Para Handy, if suddenly reintroduced to today's Clyde, would find it changed beyond all understanding. Certainly the almost complete absence of shipbuilding and of shipping traffic would astonish him, as would all the gadgetry and paraphernalia of the modern world. Yet in many respects the majority of the harbours of the Clyde have managed to retain much of their original character and atmosphere.

Campbeltown, for example, still exhibits many of the same characteristics as it had at the beginning of the century. Though its economy and its population structure may have changed, the town remains by far the most isolated community of its size in Scotland (if not indeed anywhere in the United Kingdom) and thus retains an individuality which is in marked contrast to the bland conformity which characterises more centrally-located towns with similar population numbers.

The discerning traveller – whether a genuine latter-day Phileas Fogg, or simply an armchair enthusiast – complains that the world today has shrunk to the extent that the idiosyncrasies and quirks which once distinguished one country from another have largely vanished, overwhelmed by the move towards a global conformity in everything from dress to cuisine, culture to architecture, which is largely manipulated by international commerce and investment.

That global condition is echoed in the depressing sameness of so many British towns and cities. The same hotel chains, the same high-street multiples, the same fast-food restaurants, the same garage franchises, serve a generation living in startlingly similar homes in look-alike housing estates nation-wide, products of what seems to be a common mould from Inverness to Ilfracombe, Aberdeen to Abergavenny.

On the Clyde estuary, certainly on its western shores and its islands, a significant and pleasing degree of individuality marks the towns and villages. My belief is that the river which *linked* the communities of the Clyde in Neil Munro's era – when road communication was slow and uncomfortable, and freight and people largely moved by sea – has in the period since the demise of the great steamer fleets served to *distance* them from the worst excesses of the conforming process which has swept the communities of central Scotland – and most of the rest of the United Kingdom.

Island communities have always retained their individuality by virtue of their geography: today, the absence of the steamer network has made artificial "islands" of communities like Campbeltown. That town is today linked to Glasgow only by road, all 140 miles of it, and has no direct communication with any other part of Scotland. Since that road passes through no larger community than

Campbeltown until it skirts Dumbarton, just 20 miles from its destination in Glasgow, Campbeltown really is a community in splendid isolation and with very few external influences to alter its social fabric.

Even the Cowal peninsula displays characteristics reminiscent of an island despite the fact that only a twenty minute ferry crossing, one which is in operation for 15 hours daily on a virtual shuttle basis, separates it from "mainland" Scotland. A walk along Argyll Street, Dunoon's main shopping centre, is proof of how the town has retained an individuality and an aura of self-sufficiency which have long been lost elsewhere.

The Cowal catchment population of some 12,000 is too small to attract the majority of the High Street multiples – so Argyll Street is refreshingly unlike the shopping centres of by far the majority of Scottish towns. Private, family owned businesses offer the services which in so many places have been taken over by the national chains. More, because of the very existence of the stretch of water which separates Dunoon from the mainstream economy of the central belt, the variety of retail services on offer is very wide – and the standards set are high. Since there is nowhere else for customers to go other than by taking a time-consuming ferry trip – which must also be paid for – Dunoon can support a retail network which would be the envy of towns many times its size.

The town in the years when the **Vital Spark** was plying the firth was of a very similar character to that which it retains to this day.

It was the service centre for the Cowal community – and a major holiday destination, though the majority of its patrons were the working men and women of the industrial towns and villages of Central Scotland, where today coachloads of retired couples from the North of England are the norm.

At the beginning of the last century, Dunoon had been little more than a Highland clachan with a church and manse, and a handful of thatched and slate-roofed cottages. The development of the steamer traffic on the Clyde changed all that. With the erection of the first substantial pier at Dunoon in 1835 the influx from Glasgow began. The first newcomers were the wealthy Glasgow merchants who built fine stone houses along the shores of the east and west bays – not always just as holiday and weekend retreats. The speedy service which the paddlers were able to offer meant that daily commuting to work from a home in Dunoon or the adjacent communities of Innellan, Kirn and Hunter's Quay became increasingly the norm. The answer was to make the short crossing to Gourock, or Greenock Princes Pier, to link with the regular and comfortable rail services direct to the city.

Indeed at the close of the Victorian era it was possible to travel by public transport to Glasgow from Dunoon – or Rothesay – more speedily and more conveniently than one can do so today.

By then Dunoon had grown to a population of almost 9,000 and a contemporary gazetteer described the community as "exhibiting a charming indifference to town-like regularity, villas and cottages being blended with gardens and trees." It could also remark on the town's "beautiful cemetery"!

Dunoon was by that time well-established as a major Clyde coast holiday resort, locked in rivalry for the supreme position with Rothesay – a rivalry which lasted into the 1960s, when the altered patterns of UK holiday practice and the withdrawal of so much of the steamer service on the Firth saw a decline in numbers and a significant change in the patronage of the Clyde resorts.

A large number of hotels and guest houses had been built, and in addition there were – then as now – a significant number of nursing homes as well. Paramount among these was the "Convalescent Sea-side Home", originally planned as a hydropathic, which was claiming in its advertising at the end of the Victorian era that "upwards of 48,000 patrons have been restored to health".

Shopping services were substantial, to cope with

demand from the huge influx of visitors as well as the needs of the local and hinterland communities. There were three banks – the Clydesdale, which still has a branch in the town, and the long since amalgamated British Linen and Union Banks. Imposing new burgh buildings had been completed, and there was a cottage hospital. Other services included a local gas-works, and a highly esteemed water supply.

On the cultural and social scene, the town supported no fewer than three weekly papers. There were agricultural and horticultural societies and regular horse and cattle fairs. The Cowal Gathering had been established – the first record of the event is contained in the local press in August 1894 – but it would be some years before it began to grow to its present status as the largest and most influential Highland Gathering in the world. There was a bowling club – and a golf club just recently established – and the Royal Clyde Yacht Club was in residence at Hunter's Quay, while the boatyards of Sandbank and Ardnadam on the Holy Loch were producing world-class yachts for the seriously wealthy as well as smaller craft for a more local market.

Lastly, the Dunoon of the period offered an extraordinary variety of choice for Sunday worship remarkable even in that church-going era.

There was the Church of Scotland Parish Kirk; the United Presbyterian Church; the Free Church of Scotland; the Free Gaelic Church; the Scottish Episcopal Church; and a Roman Catholic chapel. In the summer, to meet the demands of visitors from south of the border, there was a seasonal English Episcopal Church, and a Baptist Chapel.

It's doubtful if Para Handy and his crew would have made use of these church-going facilities but in any event, quite surprisingly, there is no account of the **Vital Spark** ever having touched at Dunoon, never mind spent any time there though she often sailed past.

She did, however, call at Innellan pier just three miles south of Dunoon: it was here that Dougie's wife came one Saturday morning, hunting his wages.

Para Handy's Innellan "enjoyed abundant facilities of communication with Glasgow and Rothesay through the medium of the Railway Steamers" and was already well-developed as a resort in its own right. Though the population was under one thousand, the village had its own gasworks and water supply independent of Dunoon, and a wide choice of hotels and guest houses. As well as a bowling club, Innellan also had a 9-hole golf course and a tennis club – and, given its small size, an astonishing total of four churches!

But turning away for the moment from the Cowal peninsula, there were many other Clyde harbours (with which Neil Munro would be very familiar) in which episodes from the Para Handy tales are set.

Glasgow was the puffer's port of registry, and the homes of the mate, the engineer and, after his marriage, Para Handy himself were here too. However, though she would have made many trips up and down the upper reaches of the Clyde with cargoes from or to Glasgow, it is unlikely that she would have spent very many nights or weekends lying over in the City docks.

A more usual haunt of the puffer fleets would have been farther down stream at the Dumbartonshire village of Bowling.

The village lay at the west end of the Forth and Clyde canal and had large basins much used by the various Clyde steamer fleets for berthing surplus vessels during the winter months.Bowling was also a regular port of call for the puffers. Many of them would lie there over the weekend: many of them, certainly the smaller three-man boats, themselves plied on the canal. Many indeed had been built on the canal, at the Maryhill yards of Swan and Co. or, much farther inland, at the two yards at Kirkintilloch – those of Peter MacGregor & Sons and the much larger enterprise of John Hay. As well as being builders of puffers for near on one hundred years, the company founded by John Hay in the eighteen sixties became substantially the largest operator of puffers. Most Hay vessels were instantly recognisable by their names, quite apart from their house flag and colours. They bore the so-called "tribal" names, always a single word and often a single syllable, such as **Turk, Serb, Celt, Gael, Moor, Zulu, Inca.**

Though puffers are almost invariably associated with the Clyde and its environs, they were for generations the main means of transporting goods on the canal – and indeed they traded to and from Forth ports as well.

Bowling, crossroads for puffers proceeding eastwards along the canal as well as for boats going up and down the river and putting in to berth overnight, grew up round the terminus of the waterway on a flat expanse of land lying between the river and the Kilpatrick hills. The village was notable in having the unique parallel adjacency of river – the Clyde: canal – the Forth and Clyde: railway – the Glasgow to Oban line: and roadway – the main road to the Western Highlands from Glasgow: all running alongside each other within a narrow strip of land. At the turn of the century Bowling had a small shipbuilding and ship repair yard, and a distillery. The census showed a total population of just 803, but the village had two inns and a village "Institute" with reading and billiard rooms.

The most tantalising sight which could have been seen in Bowling at the time, though one which was probably of little or no interest to those who actually had the opportunity to see it, was the fast-decaying hulk of the little paddler **Industry**, the oldest steamboat in existence. In her way a precursor, if a very early one, of the puffers themselves, **Industry** had been built at Fairlie on the Ayrshire coast in 1814 – just two years after Henry Bell's **Comet** was launched and the steam age was born. Where **Comet** was intended, and used, for passenger traffic only, **Industry** was specifically designed to carry mails and priority freight cargoes and for more than half a century she plied the river between Glasgow and Greenock before being abandoned and left to rot in the Bowling basin.

A few miles down river on the opposite side of the Clyde from Bowling the three Renfrewshire towns of Port Glasgow, Greenock and Gourock link into each other along a narrow, six-mile strip of land below the hills which rise steeply above the estuary.

"Port" Glasgow was the original Port which the city created for itself in the seventeenth century, long before there was any thought of dredging the Clyde to become a navigable river. Port Glasgow was very nearly sited at Dumbarton: the Glasgow magistrates first approached Dumbarton Council to negotiate the purchase of sufficient land to create a harbour on that side of the Clyde. Only when that approach was rejected did they look to the other Greenock side of the firth, and buy just 20-odd acres of land – a small beginning from which the prosperous town and shipbuilding centre of Port Glasgow grew.

Greenock was at its peak in the latter years of the nineteenth century. Records detail shipping movements in and out of her docks in excess of 8,000 vessels annually. The 1881 census showed it to be the fifth-largest town in Scotland, but other communities were expanding rapidly and by the turn of the century Greenock had slipped back to eighth place. It had been an important harbour since the early eighteenth century, and a major shipbuilding centre since the 1880s. Its population of approaching 70,000 was 15 times greater than neighbouring, largely residential Gourock. Today the imbalance is much less marked: Greenock, with 60,000 citizens, is just five times the size of Gourock.

Around 1900, as well as the docks and shipyards on which its commercial success had been founded, Greenock had developed an extended industrial base. Iron foundries supplied the raw materials for the yards, and marine engineering companies the power to drive the ships. But workshops also built locomotives for the growing railway networks and there were sawmills, granaries, tanneries, dyeworks, chemical factories, a pottery, a distillery, and a brewery. Next to its shipping, however, the town was best known as the country's major centre for the sugar trade, the raw material shipped home in bulk by Greenock merchantmen built in Greenock yards. There were 12 refineries in the town when the sugar trade was at its peak.

The town was also establishing itself as an entrepot for transatlantic passenger vessels with particular emphasis on the growing emigrant traffic to Canada and the United States. Greenock Princes Pier, developed to take advantage of the direct fast rail link to Glasgow city centre, was the passenger terminal for the Anchor Line among others.

Para Handy travels to Glasgow by train from Greenock and Gourock but Munro does not mention the recently-established transportation system which linked the two coastal towns – a four mile tramway skirting the foreshore and providing an electrified service from Greenock to Gourock's Ashton suburb.

Gourock was of much more recent foundation and its growth stemmed from 1889, when the Caledonian Railway opened an extension from Greenock to a new terminus at Kempock point. A new steamer pier was built (it is the one still in use today) and Gourock concentrated on becoming the Renfrewshire hub for the Clyde estuary's local passenger traffic. By the end of the century its supremacy as a steamer centre was established, the population had nearly doubled to more than 6,000, and a local guide could enthuse that "a fleet of steamers connects with the watering places on the opposite shores of the firth."

Among these were the villages scattered round Gareloch and the Holy Loch, and the remoter communities of Loch Goil and Loch Long.

In the Gareloch there were scheduled services to Rhu, Shandon, Garelochhead, Mambeg, Rahane, Rosneath, Clynder and Baremman – though these last two piers were only a quarter of a mile apart! The villages on the shore of the much smaller Holy Loch were equally well catered for, with steamer piers at Hunter's Quay, Ardnadam, Kilmun and Strone. Lochside locals hopped on and off the steamers as casually and just as matter-of-factly as today's housewives catch a bus to go the shops or businesmen a train to travel to the office.

As well as being "favourite summer residences for sea-bathers and others" there was some slight commercial activity on both lochs. Gareloch was where most of the newly-launched Clyde steamers and other coastal vessels came to undergo their time trials against the measured mile and here too their compasses were adjusted. Over in the Holy Loch puffers put in to beach and load cargoes, using the ship's winch and specially-designed grabs, at the appropriately named lochside community of Sandbank. This Loch was also, as mentioned above, a centre for the successful yacht and boat building industry on the firth.

Among the remotest Clyde communities was Arrochar, at the head of Loch Long which, with its "tributary" Loch Goil, was and still is the most "fjordlike" of all the Clyde sea-lochs. Steep and densely wooded banks close in on the water at either hand and Arrochar, in the time of the **Vital Spark**, was an isolated community of less than 600, a "row of straggling houses with one hotel" whose only direct line of communication with the outside world, apart from a railway station shared with Tarbet, Loch Lomond, was the steamer from Helensburgh. But it straddled the Glasgow to Campbeltown road and passenger and freight traffic was able to reach the village, tortuously enough in the early days, first by coach-and-horses and later by motor charabanc and lorry.

Lochgoilhead was a typically remote Highland village of the period. But even then – as now – it was a very popular holiday resort and had daily calls from steamers from Greenock and Craigendoran and, in summer, from Glasgow Bridge Wharf. There was also, for those not wishing to undertake the longer sea passage by way of the Kyles of Bute, a daily coach service through Hell's Glen and along Loch Fyneside by way of the St Catherine's ferry to Inveraray. At Lochgoilhead the visitor was beginning to impinge on the true territory of the Gael, and the 1891 census records that, of the village's 800 inhabitants, nearly half were native Gaelic speakers.

* * * * *

From the mainland shore of the firth, one popular and important destination was served, directly or indirectly, by steamers from most of its piers from Greenock south to Troon.

The Island of Arran has been particularly prized as a holiday resort by Glaswegians for generations past. The harbours of the island were frequently visited by the **Vital Spark** and her consorts for decades as well, for here was a community where every commodity and every passenger had to come in by sea.

Brodick, the principal town and steamer terminal, looked towards the Ayrshire coast. The contemporary guides enthused over its "fine, smooth beach of sand and shingle, admirably adapted for bathing" and the "sweep of plain streets, sprinkled with little hamlets, rows of cottages and pretty villages" which lay between the sea and the inland hills. There was a hotel and a public hall "with recreation rooms" and an iron steamer pier, a rare departure from the more usual wooden constructions, had been built in 1872. The resident population was little more than 1,000 but as a "favourite summer resort of families, even from the East of Scotland" this soared during the high season.

South lay the smaller resorts of Lamlash and Whiting Bay. The former possessed a fine timber pier "erected in 1884 at the expense of the Duke of Hamilton" as well as an older stone pier at which the puffers loaded or discharged their cargoes for this little community of some 300 residents. At smaller Whiting Bay there was no pier at all till 1899 and passengers travelling direct to the resort had to be put on and off shore by flit-boat. But there was a popular hotel and a number of houses to let or offering bed and board to paying guests.

There was a road right round the island, sixty miles of it, but the 1891 Gazetteer, which waxes eloquent about the magnificent panoramas of the island mountain ranges and the vistas of sea and coast to all sides, then laments that "only wild, almost impracticable footpaths lead to the sublimest views."

That road would take coach or trap traffic to Lochranza on the west side. The Campbeltown steamers also called here on both outward and inward legs of their journey. Its proximity to the herring fisheries in Kilbrannan Sound and Loch Fyne meant that Lochranza was more of a commercial community, crowded with fishing boats and temporary fishing stations in season, and with a population of almost 800.

This north end of Arran looked over to the southern coast of Bute – the fast-growing resort of Rothesay unseen on its northern coastline – and the renowned beauty spot of the sheltered Kyles which separated that island from the wilder shores of the Cowal peninsula.

By-passing Bute for the moment, the villages of the Kyles were always regular ports of call for Neil Munro's creation.

Colintraive was tiny, just "a number of pretty villas" with post office, an inn and a small steamboat pier. That pier, like so many others, has gone: but a vehicle ferry service still operates across the Kyles to Rhubodach on Bute to provide an alternative means of access to the island other than the more usual crossing from Wemyss Bay to Rothesay, and give visitors the option of a round-trip through the Cowal peninsula to Dunoon. In the immediate post-war years in the 1940s and 50s the service was inaugurated by a converted wartime landing-craft. Today Cal-Mac operate a purpose-built roll-on-roll-off vessel which completes this shortest of Clyde crossings in about three minutes flat!

In the years when the **Vital Spark** was calling at

Tighnabruaich the village was still categorised in gazetteers as a "recent watering place" but the population had climbed to over 500 and there were two hotels, a post office, the school for the other tiny Loch Ridden and neighbourhood communities – and, surprisingly, a bank. All steamers passing through the Kyles en route to Tarbert, Ardrishaig or Inveraray called at Tighnabruaich on both outward and return journeys and it became a very popular destination for a day trip from Glasgow, with passengers disembarking for several hours ashore before rejoining their steamer on its return from Loch Fyne.

Once the steamers rounded Ardlamont Point, they were in a quite different world. The communities of Loch Fyne to the north, and the Mull of Kintyre to the south, were far removed from Glasgow and the central conurbations and were thus of necessity independent in both social and economic structure.

Lying near the head of Loch Fyne, Inveraray was primarily an administrative capital. It was also Neil Munro's own birthplace and home town. The community was – and remains to this day – one of the earliest examples of structured "town planning", dating from the mid-eighteenth century when the new town was created by the Dukes of Argyll whose castle seat stands on the banks of the river Aray. Inveraray today is a neat, whitewashed town of considerable character but it was not always so interpreted by early travellers. Two nineteenth century visitors came away with very contrasting impressions. Alexander Smith thought it "a rather pretty place, with excellent inns". Robert Buchanan, on the other hand, described it as "that most depressing of fish-smelling Highland towns".

At the turn of the century it was a Royal, a Parliamentary and a Police Burgh. The County Court House had been the scene of many significant trials, none more so than that of James Stewart of Appin for the murder of Colin Campbell – the "Red Fox" – in the uneasy years after the defeat of the Jacobite troops at Culloden. Just what chance he had of a scrupulously impartial trial when he was tried on thin evidence in front of a fanatically Campbell Judge and a solidly-packed Campbell Jury for the murder of an eminent Campbell at the height of post-rebellion Clan witch-hunts can be conjectured with no difficulty. Verdict: "Guilty!"

Alongside the Court House stood a prison block with 24 cells and as well as a Police Station the town had its own gasworks and a fire-station. It was a douce, prosperous place with a choice of hotels and banks and regular cattle and wool markets. It was also the centre of the fisheries industry in upper Loch Fyne and Inveraray together with the other harbours on the shores of the loch totalled almost 400 boats employing nearly 1,000 men. Of the town's population of 1,500, more than half were Gaelic speakers.

In winter the community was linked to Glasgow by steamer three days a week: in the summer months the Glasgow and Inveraray Steamboat Company's paddler **Lord of the Isles** ran daily from Bridge Wharf. Alternatives were provided by ferry crossings to St Catherine's and Strachur, which linked to coach (later charabanc) services to Lochgoilhead and, via Loch Eck, to Dunoon and the other Cowal piers. From an early date, therefore, day visitors were offered a round trip to Inveraray – outwards by sea all the way, with an overland return, or vice versa, and this proved one of the most popular excursions on the Clyde and continued to operate well into the 1960s.

Sailing south from Inveraray, the **Vital Spark** would have been a frequent caller for cargo at the harbour of Furnace. The village was originally named for the iron-smelting works which were built there in the early nineteenth century but by Neil Munro's day the community's prosperity was largely derived from the renowned granite quarry of Dun Leacainn, first opened in 1841. There was also, located in a small glen above the village, a precursor of the trend which has continued till the present day of locating unpleasant or potentially hazardous undertakings somewhere in the Highlands in the hope that nobody will notice they are there. This was a gunpowder manufactory comprising "a number of small houses scattered over a considerable area." Though I have no record of fatal accidents at the ordnance works, there were fatalities a-plenty at the great granite quarries and Furnace became notorious for the sheer size of some of its blast-offs.

Nothing larger than a puffer could lie at the pier which served Lochgilphead. Steamers and the bigger cargo vessels berthed at Ardrishaig, two miles south. There also was the eastern entrance to the Crinan Canal, already nearly a century old. The canal could only take vessels under 90 feet in length but needless to say was a popular shortcut for the puffers, taking them out to Oban, Mull, Skye and the farther western ports without having to face the potential hazards of the stormy Mull of Kintyre. On the canal, too, MacBrayne's operated the tiny steamer **Linnet** to transfer Oban-bound passengers from the **Columba** at Ardrishaig to the **Chevalier** at Crinan.

The writer of a late Victorian gazetteer waxed lyrical about the amenities of Lochgilphead, though even he admitted that it was Ardrishaig and the adjacent canal which were the source of much of the town's prosperity. That proximity meant that Lochgilphead "shares in the growing trade of the Western Highlands, to which it owes its rise from a small fishing village to a prosperous, well-built town lighted with gas and plentifully supplied with water". There was still some fishing from Loch Gilp – though most boats were based at Ardrishaig or Tarbert, further south: and there was a textile factory. But at the time the town was best known – or most notorious – for being the location for the Mid-Argyll poorhouse, which served five neighbouring parishes: and for the sinister Argyll and Bute District Asylum for the Insane, to give its full and gory Victorian title. This institution had no fewer than 400 places in a town with a population of less than

1500! Lochgilphead is still an administrative centre to-day, housing the Headquarters of Argyll and Bute District Council.

Ardrishaig – as already indicated – was the main communications crossroads of that part of Loch Fyne. It was also much more of a commercial centre than Lochgilphead though the population was about 200 less. Huge quantities of sheep and cattle were shipped to the Glasgow markets from the lochside and hinterland crofts and farms: more than 150 fishing boats plied from the town during the main herring season: and its regular steamer schedules, with several vessels calling daily from Upper Clyde ports and Glasgow itself, had encouraged the building of a number of hotels, and consequent catering for visitors, which was much less noticeable in Lochgilphead.

The isthmus of Tarbert, south of Ardrishaig, would have been a much shorter route for a canal to the west but would have been directing traffic, once through such a waterway, back upon itself to the south west and into a much longer and more exposed sea passage north to Oban.

Several times over a period of more than one hundred years the project was however seriously considered: once by the well-respected Henry Bell, builder of the **Comet** who proposed cutting a lockless seaway similar to today's Corinth canal.: and for the last time just a decade or so before the first appearance of the **Vital Spark** in these waters, when a final proposal to build a canal capable of taking vessels substantially larger than the well-established Crinan cut could cope with fell through for lack of adequate government backing. Not a lot changes in the Western Highlands!

Tarbert village, properly East Loch Tarbert, became instead a prosperous fishing centre. The tiny East Loch is less than a mile in depth but provided a "singularly safe and landlocked natural harbour.....for a very numerous fleet of herring boats." To the substantial local fleet could be added hundreds more from all round the west coast when the herring shoals were in Loch Fyne and the Kilbrannan Sound.

By the turn of the century the village population had reached nearly 2,000 and there was a branch of the Union Bank, a Good Templar Hall (though no mention of the Rechabite Lodge which Para inadvertently joined in *Initiation [III/27]*) and four inns which, given the community's reputation as a grand place for a spree, comes as no surprise.

In summer, there were daily steamers to and from Ardrishaig, Inveraray and Glasgow and an uncomfortable coach service to and from Campbeltown. There was also an influx of long-stay visitors as well as the excursionists in their hundreds. The little town had become a "favourite seaside resort in summer" with "a number of neat cottages erected".

Just one mile across the isthmus lay the much smaller village of West Loch Tarbert, at the head of a 10 mile loch. On its banks were "a profusion of cottages, farmhouses, villas, and mansions" enjoying one of the most spectacular settings and panoramas anywhere on the west coast.

The pier at the head of the loch was the starting point for the MacBrayne steamer services to the Islay harbours of Port Askaig and Port Ellen, with connections to remoter and sparsely populated Jura.

Campbeltown, a regular port of call for the **Vital Spark,** lay in splendid isolation near the tip of the Mull of Kintyre, more than 80 miles from Glasgow by sea, almost 140 overland. The population of the parish at the turn of the century was, quite astonishingly, more than 10,000. Even today it exceeds 7,000.

Contemporary accounts portray a self-contained, confident, prosperous community which had made a virtue out of necessity by ensuring that it was as self-sufficient as possible and that like a national economy in miniature it exported more than it imported to ensure its financial stability.

The spacious harbour, sheltered by Davaar Island, could accommodate hundreds of vessels. At the height of the fishings, it had to. The Campbeltown station itself had more than 300 registered boats but, in season, the harbour was rendezvous for hundreds of fishing craft from ports throughout the United Kingdom. Onshore, to cope with the massive landings, 38 curing stations provided work for more than 800 gutters, packers and coopers. To serve the industry both afloat and ashore there were net factories, rope-walks, cooperages: at one stage there had even been salt-pans.

The harbour had three piers, and a local shipyard had been founded in 1893. The following year records show that there were 37 cargo vessels – steam and sail – registered in the name of Campbeltown owners, and the number of ships entering or leaving the harbour from or to foreign, colonial and coastal ports was nearly 2,500. Chief among the imports were barley for the local whisky industry, timber, and – in spite of the existence of a small local colliery at Drumlemble – coal. The main exports from the port were fresh and cured fish, livestock, potatoes – and of course whisky, from the 23 distilleries in the town which between them were producing in excess of two million gallons annually at the turn of the century.

Campbeltown was confident, prosperous, a "seat of considerable manufacture" set beside a bay that was "both picturesque and lively". It was, and remains today, a unique example of how a community can find success in spite of – or, some might well argue, because of its geographical situation – a situation which forces a community to look for its own success within itself, and forget any idea of hoping for external aid or the benefits of adjacency to other, larger communities from which an economic spin-off could be expected.

* * * * *

What Campbeltown most certainly *wasn't,* was a tourist centre. So, having looked in some detail at how the

Kintyre town found its prosperity in fishing, whisky and agriculture, let's close this chapter with a closer look at the turn-of-the-century state of the town which built itself up almost entirely on tourism and became the community most closely associated with the development of the holiday trade on the Clyde – Rothesay, capital of the island of Bute.

Rothesay at the turn of the century was the archetypal Clyde resort, the early twentieth century equivalent of the Spanish Costas in the seventies and eighties. Everyone went to Rothesay whether for a simple day out "doon the watter" or for a longer stay. The town was built on the prosperity that the tourist trade brought, and private sector investors, and the burgh councillors as well, ensured that facilities for visitors never stood still, but were developed, improved, extended.

At the beginning of the Victorian era, however, things had been very different. Bute in general and Rothesay in particular had been geared to industry and commerce but, for one reason or another, those enterprises which had once made the island community prosperous had all died away.

There had been four cotton mills with one thousand looms between them. First founded in the late eighteenth century, they had prospered for seventy years before going into terminal decline in the 1850s. There had been a flourishing leather industry as well, with three tanneries on the island. It too collapsed at about the same time. Two once-successful boatbuilding yards also closed. Next, local shipowners found they were being forced out of business by the aggressive marketing of the rapidly growing service provided by the Campbeltown fleets. Even the herring fisheries, which had employed (afloat and ashore) more than 2,000 men, women and boys at peak season in the eighteen fifties, were wiped out as economies of scale made it more profitable for the industry to base itself in and around the major curing centres such as – again – the burgeoning Campbeltown community.

Bute therefore had to turn to the holiday trade for the very survival of its people, and made a resounding success of it. Just ten miles from the Ayrshire and Renfrewshire coasts, just 40 miles from Glasgow – a mere hop, step and jump for the fast paddlers – the island was poised to provide the Victorian and Edwardian holidaymakers from Glasgow and the rest of Scotland with precisely what they wanted. A "different" kind of holiday option. An island with a fair climate, a fabulous setting and fun facilities of every description.

The town received an early endorsement of its tourist potential when Queen Victoria and Prince Albert berthed in the harbour in the royal yacht in 1847, and the Queen noted in her journal: "a pretty little town, built round a fine bay, with hills in the distance and a fine harbour."

That harbour was soon being extended to provide two inner basins for yachts and small craft, and a steamer quay no less than 650 feet in length to cope with the constant stream of steamer traffic which thronged the bay at the height of the season.

Ashore, private developers vied with each other in the building of bigger and better hotels. Glenburn Hydropathic, the first such in Scotland, had been opened as early as 1843 and was followed by a dozen other hotels, with guest houses and temperance establishments as well, to cater for every taste and every pocket. When the original Glenburn was destroyed by fire in 1892 it was replaced within two years on an even grander scale than before.

By the eighteen seventies the council had taken a four acre foreshore site and created on it a broad esplanade and ornamental gardens. Further esplanades were built outwards round both sweeps of the bay. The elegant winter gardens were built adjacent to the main harbour, and other amenities added in the seventies and eighties of last century included salt water swimming baths, beach bathing facilities "for ladies and gentlemen", with attended dressing rooms, and screened from the public view. A concert room was erected in 1876, along with an aquarium which included a 90 foot corridor of fish tanks, a seal house, and a *camera obscura*. In 1882 a tramway was opened to carry visitors to the quiet sands of Port Bannatyne bay three miles away – first horse-drawn, later electrified and in 1905 extended to Ettrick Bay on the West coast. Bandstands went up, and the streets and squares were decorated with statues and fountains. There were yacht clubs, an aquatic club, bowling, tennis, golf and cricket. Boat-hirers' stances were prominent along the foreshore. Three weekly papers were augmented in the summer season by the weekly *Visitors' List*.

In short, Rothesay in Para Handy's time was as prosperous and as confident in its own way – and its own way was through catering for holidaymakers – as Campbeltown was by virtue of its solid industrial and commercial base.

"Its history," says a contemporary gazetteer, "is the account of the rise, progress and decline of its commerce – and its arrival at its present position as a favourite watering-place and tourist-centre....[on which] Rothesay depends for its prosperity almost entirely."

Well-travelled visitors settled into their hotels and compared Rothesay favourably and enthusiastically with Naples for scenery, Madeira for climate. Day trippers cleared the smut and smog of the cities from their lungs as the steamers sped down river, and flocked to sample the amenities of "sweet Rothesay Bay".

"From the town and harbour," wrote one visitor, "there stretches on either side, round the entire circuit of the bay, a curving line of elegant villas, picturesquely set with their gardens and shrubberies against a background of trees" – a reminder that, as well as visitors, Rothesay was attracting permanent residents too: wealthy Glasgow merchants and professional men building summer, weekend or retirement homes, as well as others who commuted daily via Wemyss Bay and by express train into the city.

Of all the ports into which the **Vital Spark** coughed

her wheezy way, this was the one founded most firmly on the amenities of its infrastructure and its surroundings. Dunoon ran it close but Rothesay was the exemplary holiday resort par excellence on the Clyde.

Like all the other harbours on the estuary – and this chapter has been able to consider only a few – it had its own distinct characteristics. As a contrast to the working way-of-life which was the lot of most of those who spent their lives on the estuary, it seems appropriate to end this account of some of the Clyde towns and villages with a glance at what was clearly the most sybaritic of them all – Rothesay.

It was a place of escape from the realities of the working world which lured the city-dwelling Victorians and Edwardians down the firth in their tens of thousands, and first introduced many of them to the unique world of the Clyde – its people, its shipping, its sailors: a world which Neil Munro conjures up so vividly in the pages of the Para Handy stories.

CHAPTER 2

Clyde steamers and other river vessels

SHIPS and boats of every description sail across the pages of the Para Handy stories. The **Vital Spark** may be the star of the show, but there is an extensive and varied supporting cast. Indeed, given the emptiness of the Clyde Estuary now, it is hard to imagine the extent of the traffic on the river and the sheer number of vessels large and small which went about their business there. Athough, by the standards of today, the Clyde was still a busy waterway into the nineteen fifties, an era which many can still recall, the traffic even at that time was but a trickle compared with the volume in the early years of this century.

So wide is the canvas on which Neil Munro deploys the ships of his age – by name, whether real or imaginary: and by type – that it makes sense to divide them into two broad categories and consider them separately.

First, in this chapter, a look at the vessels which were native to or largely confined to the Clyde Estuary.

And in the following chapter, some account of the ships and maritime traffic from the oceans of the world which put in their appearance on the pages of the narrative.

* * * * *

Many of the vessels which feature in the tales were peculiar to the West coast of Scotland. The Clyde steamers: the Clyde Ferries: the coasting cargo vessels: the (then huge) Clyde fishing fleets: the great yachts: and of course the puffers themselves. Most, sadly, have gone for ever.

The decade before the First World War saw the volume of seaborne passenger and freight traffic on the Clyde Estuary reach levels we can scarcely credit today.

From Bridge Wharf in Glasgow down to Campbeltown on the Kintyre peninsula, or up the deep sea lochs to isolated communities such as Arrochar, Lochgoilhead and Strachur, there were more than 80 piers catering for passenger vessels alone. The largest of these, such as Princes Pier at Greenock, or those at Gourock, Craigendoran and Rothesay, had berths for up to half-a-dozen vessels, and they were in constant use. On the eve of the War, eight different steamship companies were operating no fewer than 40 large passenger vessels on the river with a network of services criss-crossing the estuary.

In addition, there were umpteen local ferry services provided by smaller craft. These ranged from the highly organised Clutha services on the upper reaches of the Clyde to the more haphazard loch and island ferries run by individual private operators.

Freight traffic between Glasgow and the ports and harbours throughout the estuary was at an equally substantial level. Many of the steamer piers "doubled" as berthing-places for cargo vessels, though the larger ports-of-call usually had separate facilities for freight traffic.

In addition, many communities which lacked any sort of pier or jetty were served – in terms of freight transportation – by the puffers. One of their attributes, one for which (with their flat bottoms) they had been specifically designed, was the ability to beach at high tide and then load or unload their cargos to or from carts and wagons as they lay high-and-dry on the ebb. The puffers were the Clyde's equivalent of the ocean-going tramp ship, sailing wherever and whenever they could find work, carrying cargoes which the larger vessels could not or would not handle, serving ports-of-call where bigger ships could not or would not go.

But as well as the puffers, there were many other

designated cargo vessels plying on the river – larger, faster and operating a scheduled service to a time-table.

One further broad class of vessel contributed to the stream of local traffic on the Clyde Estuary.

Fishing boats of all sizes plied their trade from dozens of communities, ranging from such major centres as Tarbert on Loch Fyne or Campbeltown to remote settlements which could muster but one or two inshore craft. The years of the Para Handy stories were the years of the decline of the once fabulous Loch Fyne herring fisheries but there were still hundreds of boats of every description hauling a living from the sea.

All this, remember, was traffic peculiar to the Clyde, based in it and working in it. But it was at this period, too, that other, external traffic was also at its zenith. The Clyde was choc-a-bloc with ocean-going vessels and the upper reaches of the river had become a major seaport and entrepot for international freight (and, to a somewhat lesser extent, passenger) traffic.

Between 1880 and 1920 the available berthing space in the Clyde docks increased more than three-fold: the cargo tonnage landed or exported went up 500 per cent. Coal shipments alone averaged about 5,000,000 tons annually over the period covered by the Para Handy stories.

At this period too the Clyde was approaching its zenith as the unchallenged world leader in shipbuilding, in yards which were household names worldwide for decades. Tonnages launched rose from totals of less than 400,000 tons in 1880 to more than 1,500,000 in 1900.

* * * * *

In common with most of the various types of vessel which appear in the pages of the books, the Clyde steamers, naturally, were built on the Clyde in Scottish-owned yards. They were built to a timescale – and at a price – which seem quite beyond belief today, particularly since there was little mechanisation and most work was the product of blood, sweat, toil and tears.

David MacBrayne's crack paddler **Grenadier** was built in 1885 at the Clydebank Yard of J. & G. Thomson – 222 feet in length, and fitted out to the highest standards – for a contract price of just £15,900. She sailed the winter mail service for MacBrayne on the key Glasgow-Ardrishaig route.

Ten years later the same yard built the **Duchess of Rothesay** for the Caledonian Steam Packet Co. Generally recognised to have been one of the loveliest of all the Clyde paddlers, she was in service for more than fifty years, and requisitioned by the Admiralty in both World Wars. She was significantly bigger, and faster, than the **Grenadier** yet ten years on (an interesting commentary on comparative rates of inflation) she cost just £4,000 more. What is more astonishing still, perhaps, is that her keel was laid down in December 1894, the hull was launched in April 1895, she ran her trials four weeks later, and was in service before the end of May!

So much has been written – and so well – about the steamers and so much is still in print that it would seem superfluous to go into too much detail about them in a book which does not claim to a specialist knowledge of such a deeply-researched subject. This is intended as an overview of a lost world, and not as a thesis on specifics. But the Clyde passenger steamers have become a legend and there is reason for believing that they even were so regarded in their own lifetime.

By the late 1940s and early 1950s, which is the period in which most of those with a personal experience of those little ships had that experience, the steamers' role as the network freight and passenger lifeline of the estuary was largely over. There were some exceptions, of course, and there are still some even today. For the islanders of Arran, Bute and Cumbrae, and to a lesser extent for the residents of the Cowal peninsula, sea transport is the essential common element which keeps their communities alive.

But in Munro's days, the complete fabric of life of the entire Clyde Estuary was dependent on sea communications. Roads were rough and ready but, above all, rural road transport was still much of a horse and cart affair. The motor vehicle was very much in the minority. There were few cars, fewer goods lorries, fewest of all buses or charabancs. People and goods, and of course the mail service, were more often than not moved by sea. Not only was such a passage much quicker – a glance at the map of the estuary will show how tortuous some of the land-links are – it was also a great deal more comfortable. Provided the weather stayed fair!

The importance of MacBrayne's flagship route from Glasgow to Ardrishaig, maintained on a daily basis year round by the company's finest and fastest vessels, was that it provided the most agreeable and the speediest access to Oban, the Highlands and the Western Islands from any departure point in southern Scotland and the whole of England. A relatively short road journey from Ardrishaig, or a sheltered sailing passage through the Crinan Canal and north by way of the Firth of Lorne, linked passengers and mail (and to a lesser degree high-value freight cargo too) to Oban and the complex steamer network which served the Western Islands and Highlands from that busy port.

The Crinan Canal was already 100 years old. Since it had been designed to give passage to the type of craft operating at the time it was constructed, by Para Handy's day only very small passenger vessels, fishing boats, and of course puffers, could use a canal whose locks could not accommodate anything whose hull was more than 90 feet in length.

Therefore bulk freight, and passengers wishing to travel direct to Oban and the Western Islands without change of transport in the process, had to face the long and often stormy haul round the Mull of Kintyre.

As the nineteenth century closed, gradually – very gradually – tourists from farther afield were beginning to rival local traffic in importance on the steamers of the Clyde, at least in the summer months. Nevertheless it would be many years before the development of road transport first dominated and then destroyed the older, water-borne freight services to the lochside towns and villages: before the river ceased to be almost the sole means of passenger transport from remote communities to the main ports of the estuary and of course to Glasgow itself: or before the ubiquitous Glaswegians stopped flooding down river in the summer months to make the Clyde Coast the greatest holiday destination not just in Scotland, but in the British Isles.

Those years at the turn of the century were the high days of a unique transportation network. Its place in history and in the affections even of those who never saw it at its peak is assured by virtue of the means by which it was delivered, and the nostalgia with which the steamers that provided it will for all time be associated.

Of the other types of vessel which feature in the tales, the puffers are obviously the stars and deserve (and get) a chapter to themselves.

Gabbarts are regularly referred to. These were small coastal sailing vessels, in effect the predecessors of the puffers, and were largely obsolescent by the time of the Para Handy stories. The **Katharine-Anne,** abandoned by her Tighnabruaich owner and crew and salvaged by the **Vital Spark** in a storm off Ettrick Bay, was one such vessel. The **Sara,** crewed by Para Handy and Dougie in the years before they took their places on the **Vital Spark,** was another. They were broad-beamed, flat-bottomed, single-masted and clumsy to handle. Para Handy, as loyal to his earlier command as he was to the puffer which became the love of his life, might claim that the **Sara** "when she had the wind on her quarter and her sails mended would go like a man-of-war" – but then he would, wouldn't he!

The "Cluthas" were working vessels of a very different type, a kind of water-borne Public Service Vehicle which ran on the very upper reaches of the river from the mid-1880s. There had been small cross-river ferries (as well as the larger freight ferries) at several points on the upper river for many years, carrying passengers from one bank to the other. The new service provided an up-and-down-river routing, with ten points of call (on both sides of the Clyde) in the course of a four mile run from Stockwell Street Bridge, in the heart of Glasgow, to Whiteinch, downriver from Govan.

At one time there were twelve of the little vessels on the route, providing a shuttle service up and down the river. They were really Clyde steamers in miniature, with seated saloons below deck, and the largest able to carry more than 300 passengers. It was the improvement to the road transport – in this case the successful introduction of electric trams – which put paid to them, just as it eventually put paid to almost all of the marine traffic on the Clyde. At the height of their brief lifespan though, in the mid-nineties, the little boats carried more than 2 million passengers annually. But decline was swift and irreversible, and the last Clutha was withdrawn from service in 1903.

Since we know that Sunny Jim – who makes his first appearance in the opening episode of *In Highland Harbours* – had previously been a deckhand on the Cluthas, that would seem to be reasonable evidence for suggesting that the stories in *The Vital Spark* are set prior to that date.

Small coastal sailing vessels were still very common in the days of the **Vital Spark.** They ranged in size from the gabbarts already discussed, which were strictly for estuary use, to the larger inshore barges, ketches, schooners and other rigs which carried coals to Newcastle – and any other cargo they could lay their hands on.

These too became victims of steam – of the two-island and three-island coasters, with engines aft, which plied the ports of Britain well into the fifties and early sixties. Land transport finally did for them too, as it has done for almost all local seaborne traffic other than the vital links to our island communities.

Long before the virtual demise of those sea-going coasters, however, the smaller steam cargo vessels which served the nooks and crannies of the Clyde with a proper, scheduled service – as against the random "tramping" of the puffers – had long been forced out of business.

Three real ships which provided that crucial service in Munro's days appear periodically in the stories and can be considered together.

The smallest was the **Texa**, launched from Scott & Co.'s Bowling yard in 1884. At just 100 ft. overall – though later lengthened to 118 ft. – she was really little more than a big brother to the puffers themselves. She was a screw steamer, with engines aft, and though Sunny Jim arrived on her at Rothesay to join the **Vital Spark** it is unlikely that she ever carried passengers other than, perhaps, the occasional seaman or commercial traveller. The description *(A New Cook [II/1])* of the cargo to be seen in her hold gives a splendid glimpse of the variety of the freight traffic on the Clyde! "It held nothing maritime – only hay-bales, flour-bags, soap-boxes, shrouded mutton carcases, rolls of plumbers' lead, two head-stones for Ardrishaig, and the dismantled slates, cushions and legs of a billiard-table for Strachur."

Her first five years were on the Islay route, but thereafter she spent most of her life on MacBrayne's Loch Fyne service before being sold to an Isle of Man company in 1917.

The **Cygnet,** built for MacBrayne by Inglis of Pointhouse in 1904, was a slightly larger vessel at 135 ft. overall and she did have some (very limited) designated passenger facilities. She and **Texa** worked the Ardrishaig route together till the latter was sold on. At that time, too, **Cygnet** herself was transferred to Oban and operated what was primarily a freight-only service to Coll, Tiree, Castlebay and Lochboisdale. She was finally scrapped in 1930.

The largest of this trio was the **Minard Castle,**

Clyde-built by Fullerton's in 1882 for the Lochfyne & Glasgow Steam Packet Co Ltd, which ran a Glasgow to Inveraray service.

She was a small three-island screw steamer, 140 ft. overall, with two tall masts and a generally pleasing appearance, with modest accommodation for a few passengers. She went to the breakers in Port Glasgow in 1926.

* * * * *

The years of the **Vital Spark** were also the hey-day of the great racing yachts. *Among the Yachts [II/16]* contains a fine eye-witness account of a race which develops into a duel of wits between the old rivals **White Heather** and one of Sir Thomas Lipton's America's Cup challengers – **Shamrock.** Between 1899 and 1930 Sir Thomas fielded five yachts carrying that name in a gallant but vain attempt to win the trophy for Britain for the first time ever.

It is almost certain that the **Shamrock** described in the story was the third to carry the name: her unsuccessful challenge was made in 1903 but the American sloop **Reliance** bested her to retain the trophy for the United States.

To call these boats "great yachts" is neither overstatement nor figure-of-speech. They were classed as forty metre racers: 130 feet overall, nearly twice the length of the **Vital Spark** herself, and very much the plaything and the indulgence of the seriously rich. It would be many years before yacht racing reduced in scale (and expense) to come within reach of the less affluent. Lipton's fortune came from grocery and teas: other protagonists in the Scottish racing scene included the immensely wealthy Coats family whose Paisley thread fortunes financed two of the yachts – **Hera** and **Pallas** – which are participants in the race Munro described.

Cost and size apart, another factor which differentiates yacht racing then and now is that, in Para Handy's days, the owners of the yachts did not often skipper them in competition. They funded them, commissioned them, and watched them perform. But their performance in racing situations was frequently left in the hands of professional crews.

What further distinguishes the actual America's Cup races of Para Handy's times from those of today is that what was till 1958 a contest of Forty Metre giants is now, in recognition of changed financial realities, fought out by yachts of half that size.

A nice touch in Munro's story is that the real aficionado of the yachts with their grace, glamour and speed is Engineer Dan MacPhail. The man who presides over the most asthmatic and least reliable engines afloat in the West of Scotland, the man for whom seven knots is an unattainable dream, is the man with the enthusiasm and love for the white-winged racers, driving the puffer to her limit in order to reach the Gareloch in time to see the finish.

"MacPhail was stoking carefully and often, like a mother feeding her first baby..... keeping his steam at the highest pressure short of blowing off the safety valve, on which he had tied a pig-iron bar..... her bows were high out of the water and she left a wake astern of her like a liner."

Even Para Handy shows a suspiciously knowledge-able interest in the yachts about which he pretends such contempt – "where would we be withoot oor coal-boats: look at them chaps sprauchlin' on the deck" – and then reveals that he spent a season or two on them in his younger days: "no a bad job at aal, but aawful hurried..... I would chust as soon be in a lawyer's office."

* * * * *

The most regular appearances on Munro's Clyde canvas however are those of the Clyde Steamers them-selves. Now an all but extinct breed they were, thankfully, recorded for posterity in words and music, on film and in art – and surely rank amongst the most beautiful artefacts ever created by man.

Some were boats of quiet history and little glory though no less interesting for that. But as we would expect there are starring roles for those ships that were recognised as classics in their own day just as surely as they are remembered as legends in our own.

Most venerable of them all was the **Inveraray Castle.** She was a clipper-bowed paddler, the very first vessel to be launched from Tod & McGregor's new Partick yard in 1839. She spent her entire, long working life carrying two generations of freight and passengers on the Glasgow to Inveraray service, passing through the hands of various owners before she was finally broken up in 1895. She was twice back at the builders to have her hull lengthened, an operation which was carried out quite frequently in the Victorian years. Launched at 136 feet, she was extended to 158 feet in 1862 and to 173 feet eleven years later.

She was very much a utilitarian boat, with many isolated ports of call for the discharge of cargo: the run from Glasgow to Inveraray took her a full day and she lay overnight at the Loch Fyne harbour before retracing her journey to Glasgow the following morning.

Para Handy relates that he was a deckhand on her with MacBrayne's in *The Maids of Bute [II/19]:* this must have been after 1879, prior to which date the owners traded under the Hutcheson name, but before 1890 when she was laid up at Bowling. The developing tourist potential of upper Loch Fyne in the eighties made the introduction of faster and more luxurious vessels inevitable, and the demise of the old workhorses equally so.

Speed and comfort had always been a hallmark of the crack ships which provided the service on MacBrayne's blue riband Glasgow to Ardrishaig route, the most prestigious of all the Clyde services and one which survived till the very last days of the steamers in the 1960s.

Probably the most famous and certainly the most spectacular of the many ships which served the route in its century of operation was Macbrayne's **Columba,** built by

J. & G. Thomson at Clydebank and launched in 1878.

One can sympathise with Para Handy's fury at the impertinence of the urchins who yelled "**Columba** ahoy!" at the passing **Vital Spark.** No two vessels could present a greater contrast!

The MacBrayne flagship was the largest steamer ever to operate on the Clyde. She was 301 ft. overall and could carry 2,000 passengers.

(It has to be admitted that Cal-Mac's latest Arran ferry, the mv **Caledonian Isles,** which came into service in August 1992, is seven feet longer. But she carries only half the passenger numbers and, in any case, there are those of us who would suggest that she just "doesn't count" in comparison with the most famous vessel the Clyde fleets ever spawned.)

Columba's service speed of 21 knots was never exceeded and was not even equalled till the launch of the turbine steamer **Queen Alexandra** 24 years later. The luxury of her interiors staggered even the wealthy Victorians for whom she catered. The woods used to panel her public rooms included teak, maple, mahogany and rosewood. There was a conservatory leading off the principal saloon which itself was more than 80 feet long.

She had a post office, a barber's shop, full bathrooms (which boasted silver-plated fittings) for the refreshment and comfort of passengers who had travelled to Glasgow on the overnight train from London. Her dining saloon, for the first time, introduced the concept of individual tables for parties and families, rather than the communal board which had been the practice till then. There was a constant round-the-clock catering service while she was on passage, with a choice of up to 15 different hot dishes on the menu.

And the **Vital Spark**? In her skipper's own words *(Para Handy, Master Mariner [I/1]):* "She is aal hold, with the boiler behind, four men and a derrick, and a watter-butt and a pan loaf in the fo'c'sle." But he could dream......"Oh man! she wass the beauty! She wass chust sublime! She should be carryin' nothing but gentry for passengers, or nice genteel luggage for the shooting-lodges, but there they would be spoilin' her and rubbin' all the pent off her with their coals, and sand, and whunstone, and oak bark, and timber, and trash like that."

The **Columba** ran a punishing summer schedule. Her role was to provide the crucial link from Glasgow – via a series of intermediate Clyde ports-of-call – which carried passengers and the mails to link with the onward services to Islay and Jura, and to Oban and all points west and north. While much steamer traffic on the Clyde remained local traffic, from the beginning **Columba** and the other big paddlers on the Ardrishaig run were providing a through service largely patronised by the more affluent members of Scottish society, including Highland landowners and their guests – and an ever-growing number of tourists.

MacBrayne's published timetable saw the **Columba** or the **Iona** or one of her cohorts leave Bridge Wharf in the centre of Glasgow at 7.00 a.m. After calling en route at Greenock, Gourock, Dunoon, Innellan, Rothesay, Colintraive, Tighnabruaich, Tarbert (where passengers for Islay transferred across the isthmus to where another MacBrayne vessel awaited them at West Loch Tarbert) she arrived at Ardrishaig, 83 miles from Glasgow, at 12.40 p.m. The paddler began her return journey 20 minutes later and reached Bridge Wharf at 6.30 that evening.

Meanwhile, passengers for Oban and beyond were offered two alternatives.

They could leave Ardrishaig by small boat, usually the **Linnet,** along the Crinan Canal, reaching the Atlantic seaboard at 2.55 p.m., where the MacBrayne paddler **Chevalier** waited to whisk them to Oban by 4.50 p.m.

Those of a less nautical inclination could proceed by coach and horses (MacBrayne's bought their first motor bus in 1907) to the village of Ford at the southern end of Loch Awe – just over two hours for the 14 miles of road journey. At Ford they embarked on the Loch Awe steamer and at 5.10 p.m. arrived at the pier at Loch Awe village, thirty miles to the north. With the self-confidence common to the late Victorians and Edwardians, the timetable allowed just five minutes for the passengers to connect with the Glasgow to Oban railway at Loch Awe Village station – and the by then presumably pretty exhausted travellers finally arrived at Oban at 6.15 p.m.

Since the journey to Oban (though not to Ardrishaig, of course) could be completed more swiftly and with much less stress by simply electing to take the train direct from Glasgow, those passengers choosing to travel this route must be seen as early pioneers of tourism in the west, for whom how one travelled and through what sort of scenery took precedence over mere speed and convenience.

Indeed, following the introduction of **Columba** on the Ardrishaig service in 1878, MacBrayne's promoted the round trip to the Loch Fyne port assiduously as a day excursion from Glasgow for visitors and Scots alike. Since almost all their other routes lay in the farther north west, (though they did their utmost to create attractive week-long excursions constructed around them), only on the Ardrishaig run did they have the opportunity to tap directly into the bulk market that the main population centres, and the principal Clyde resort traffic, could offer.

The "day out", involving just thirty minutes short of twelve hours aboard and passing through the finest scenery the Clyde had to offer, cost – in 1888 – just 2/6 (12p) in second and 4/- (20p) in first class, or fore-cabin and cabin as they were known on board.

Nearly a quarter of a century later, in 1911, those fares had risen only to 4/- (20p) and 6/- (30p) respectively: and for a total of just 4/- (20p) extra in second and 4/6 (22p) in first, passengers could enjoy a package of three full meals – breakfast, lunch and high tea – in the ship's renowned dining saloons, spending the rest of the passage at rest in the comfort of the generous and beautifully fitted saloons or, in fine weather, strolling the decks.

This was the kind of ambiance that poor Para Handy longed to believe was attached to the **Vital Spark,** and these wealthy passengers were the kind of cargo for which he dreamed the puffer had really been created and for which she was best suited.

And what did he have to put up with in reality? The heartless indifference of most of his crew – and the unfeeling teasing of the Glasgow youngsters who watched his painful progress up and down the river.

No wonder the **Columba** jibes hurt!

That remarkable ship remained in service on the Clyde for almost 60 years, finally going to the breakers in 1936.

Of three other MacBrayne steamers featured, the **Claymore** was not in fact one of the Clyde fleet. She operated on the Oban to Mull service, and appears in the story of the stranded whale *(Treasure Trove [II/4])* when the puffer makes one of her occasional sorties out of the Firth. Another product of the Thomson yard, **Claymore** was built in 1881 and scrapped exactly half a century later.

The **Grenadier,** which Thomson's launched for MacBrayne four years later, divided her year between the Clyde and the Western Isles. She was another classic and highly-regarded MacBrayne vessel – a handsome, clipper-bowed paddler with a prominent bowsprit providing her with an unmistakable silhouette. For much of her working life she spent the summer months sailing out of Oban: first to Mull, Skye and north to Gairloch in Wester Ross: latterly with excursion parties to Staffa and Iona. In winter, she returned to the Clyde to operate on the Glasgow-Ardrishaig run. The simple economics of that route were that it was at its most profitable only in summer months, when the landowners and wealthy visitors patronised it as they moved north to their Highland estates. In winter it reverted to much more of a local service, and it would have been hopelessly uneconomical to use ships like the **Columba** to carry a much smaller passenger and freight load.

It says something about the commercial profligacy, or perhaps more likely about the profit margins, of the Victorian shipping industry that operators like MacBrayne could afford to build a vessel like the **Columba** – and use her for less than six months each year, laying her up to overwinter at the Bowling basin.

Grenadier was the only MacBrayne paddler to be employed on active service during the First World War. She was re-named **HMS Grenade** and worked as a minesweeper in the North Sea.

She survived the war, but came to a tragic end in peace-time. A fire broke out in the early hours of September 6, 1927, as she lay berthed overnight at Oban. It quickly took hold and the ship, so much of her construction being of highly flammable wood, was a burnt-out shell. The majority of the crew were able to escape but two crew members, and her captain, died in the disaster.

The handsome **Lord of the Isles** was built in 1891 for the Glasgow & Inveraray Steamboat Co. Ltd. by D. & W. Henderson, Partick. She was targeted very much at the upper end of the market, luxuriously fitted out to appeal to the wealthy tourist rather than the day-trip excursionist. She ran daily from Glasgow to Inveraray and return with no fewer than 10 intermediate ports of call on both legs of the journey. Later in life she provided a "round Bute" service calling at Tighnabruaich in the Kyles, and during the war she operated the Lochgoilhead route. She was broken up in 1928.

* * * * *

This brief look at the Clyde vessels of Para Handy's age ends appropriately with one of the most truly pioneering vessels of all time. The skipper of the **Vital Spark** may have pretended not to notice when the **King Edward** went by him "like a streak of lightning" but here was a ship which set the stage for a whole new chapter in world maritime history.

This beautiful vessel remained in service for half-a-century and since she was scrapped only in 1951 there are still thousands who sailed her, myself included, and who remember her well and with much affection. She truly was a direct link with the golden years of the Clyde.

The concept of the turbine engine was the invention of Charles Parsons. It was a concept which would revolutionise marine engineering. In simplest terms, turbine engines are more efficient because they drive the screws by direct rotary motion rather than by the complex reciprocating linkages of piston and crankshaft. And they are more effective – delivering greater power and speed at lower cost.

The very first experimental turbine engine was installed in the little yacht **Turbinia** in 1897. She made her first public appearance by cheekily gate-crashing Queen Victoria's Jubilee Review of the Grand Fleet at Spithead in 1897. The episode is deliberately parodied by the **Vital Spark**'s appearance among the naval and merchant vessels assembled on the Clyde to celebrate the centenary, in 1912, of the launch of the **Comet** – recognised as the original pioneer of commercial maritime steam. *[BP/85]*

Back in real life at Spithead in 1897, however, not even the fastest vessels of the assembled naval might could keep up with, never mind catch, the impudent infiltrator which weaved in and out of the lines of battleships and destroyers.

Parsons had made his point. His new turbine engine could not be ignored; the Admiralty took it up, and within three years two experimental naval vessels had been built with turbine engines. They achieved speeds in excess of 37 knots – an unimaginable achievement for those days. However, a turbine engine had yet to be installed in an ordinary commercial vessel. The Clyde – and a Clyde steamer – showed the way.

In 1901 the triple-screw steamer **King Edward** was launched at Dumbarton for a consortium comprising Parsons' own company, William Denny the builders, and

Captain John Williamson who would operate her.

This beautiful ship had a service speed of 20 knots – modest by comparison with the naval prototypes but enough to outrun anything else then on the Clyde with the exception of the **Columba,** and delivered economically and efficiently. She was therefore placed on the longest routes. Glasgow to Campbeltown and return: Glasgow to Inveraray and return: Glasgow to Bute and Arran.

She saw service in both wars. In the First she was employed as an ambulance transport, and deployed on one occasion as far as Archangel, though much of her work was much closer to home, cross-channel to France as it was in the Second War as well.

King Edward returned to the Clyde in 1946, operating between Glasgow and the Kyles, with occasional excursions to Arran. She was laid up at the end of the 1951 season and, sadly, the decision was taken to scrap her and she went to the breakers the following year.

From the **Inveraray Castle** of 1839 to the **King Edward** of 1901. Generations apart in time, in style, in performance – but Para Handy and his crew saw them all, and Neil Munro shares them with us, a four-dimensional cross-section of the history of the small ships on the Clyde.

* * * * *

What is left on the river today to remind us of them? In a sense, the wheel has come full circle. Steamship operations on the Clyde were started, last century, to provide a necessary working service to the communities on the estuary, the islands and the lochs. Gradually that service became less utilitarian, more allied to what today would be called the leisure industry.

Now in the 1990s the only services left (with one notable and most welcome exception) are those catering exclusively for the essential day-to-day needs of the island communities, and the shuttle-service between Gourock and Dunoon which can be looked on as a necessary "bridge-equivalent" facility essential to social and commercial communications between the communities on opposite sides of the firth.

These are efficient and busy services, carried out by car ferries specially designed to perform effectively on a year round basis and in virtually all weathers. But, with great respect to the designers and the crews, nobody could call these ferries things of beauty. They are working vessels with few pretensions to style and they have nothing of the panache and character of the vessels they replace.

However, one last remaining ship does, for a few fleeting summer weeks, manage to turn the clock back to give today's generation just the merest glimpse of the glory days.

She is the **PS Waverley**, the last sea-going paddle steamer afloat in the world today.

She was launched – and where else could have been more appropriate than a slipway which had given birth to generations of the cream of the Clyde fleet – from A. & J. Inglis' Pointhouse yard in 1947 for the LNER, the last of the long line of Clyde paddlers. (One final, much smaller paddle steamer, would emerge from the Pointhouse yard –the 500 ton **Maid of the Loch**, built in 1953 for service on Loch Lomond, still afloat though unused for years, in need of £2 million-worth of overall restoration and with a very uncertain future.)

On the Clyde, **Waverley** marked the end of an era. That she was handed over to the Paddle Steamer Preservation Society when she was withdrawn from service in 1973 was a miracle of bureaucratic wisdom. Twenty years on, she is still giving pleasure to thousands every summer, running down a strangely quiet and deserted river from the upper reaches to the Kyles and beyond.

What is even more miraculous, though, is that **Waverley**, as well as being the last of the great paddlers, is one of the most handsome ships ever launched for the Clyde service. Given the changes to naval architecture in the half-century since she was put on the drawing-board, she is something of a time-warp and stepping aboard her is a step into history. Teak and polished brass mark her decks and saloons: and nothing in the world can thrill in quite the same way as the sight and sound of the great three cylinder engine powering the wheels, and the pervasive, intoxicating smell of hot oil.

So, even in the 1990s, it is still possible on occasion to hear the unmistakable beat of paddle wheels on the Clyde and, from the shores of the Kyles, to see the **Waverley** sweep majestically into view, that evocative sound echoing off the surrounding hills: and to conjure up a faint hint of what the Clyde must have looked like and sounded like when the **Vital Spark** was going about her business on the waters of the Firth.

CHAPTER 3

A World of Ships and Shipping

When Para Handy sailed the Firth, the Clyde Estuary was seen by readers of Neil Munro's newspaper columns as the very hub of world shipping.

The yards which lined both banks of the river – and of its principal tributaries, such as the Kelvin and the Cart – built the ocean-going craft which founded fortunes in trade for the great Scottish shipping family dynasties.

The wealth of the world, its raw materials and its manufactured goods, poured into and out of the warehouses which crowded the miles of quays created and developed by the Clyde Port Authority. This was the zenith of Glasgow as Merchant City and fortunes were being made in commodity trading by the likes of the tobacco, whisky, steel, coal and sugar barons: and by the pioneers and inventive entrepreneurs who turned the city and its catchment areas into a world centre of manufacturing innovation in everything from textiles to heavy machinery, from automobiles to chemicals.

Both as a creator of ships, and as a crew member for them, the Scottish working man was held in respect the world over. The country's reputation meant that those acquired skills were in demand in all quarters of the globe. Shipowners poured orders into the yards which had made "Clyde-built" a universally respected, not to say envied, touchstone of quality, value and reliability.

The machine-shops which peppered the river banks pioneered and produced the finest marine engines in the world. Many of the best-known shipbuilding yards had actually started life as an engine shop to serve building slipways to which they became rivals: later diversifying into construction themselves, they included the Pointhouse yard of brothers Anthony and John Inglis, builders of such Clyde notables as the **Talisman** of 1896, **Kenilworth** of 1898, **Waverley** of 1899, **Marmion** of 1906, and of course the second **Waverley** in 1947.

The crowded tenements of Govan and Plantation, Greenock and Port Glasgow, Partick and Yoker, Dumbarton and Clydebank, all provided the skilled craftsmen not just to make the ships – but to man them as well.

It was as marine engineers that the Scots really excelled and such was the demand for their services from every maritime nation that it used to be said that you could open the engine-room hatch on any ship in any port in the world and shout "Hey, Jock!" into the hidden depths – and someone would answer with an "Aye?"

As well as the technological pioneering of its shipbuilders and marine engineers, the committed investment of its merchants and importers, and the skills of its individual workmen, the Clyde's rise to dominance in world shipbuilding and to a position of power in maritime commerce in the United Kingdom depended on one other crucial factor.

The major problem of the silting of the upper reaches of the river had to be first contained and then reversed: and then, if the Clyde were to prosper as an international trading centre, docks and quays of the necessary quality and quantity must be created.

John Riddell's comprehensive history of the work of the Clyde Navigation Trust chronicles the transformation of a narrow and shallow stream into a major ocean terminal able not merely to cope with building and launching ships, but with accepting them as paying customers when they and a myriad others returned fully-laden with the wealth of the world. That transformation was achieved by constant and ever more efficient dredging operations, and by massive investment in infrastructure.

When the Victorian era began, available technology limited dredging activity to depths of around 14 feet. By the time of the **Vital Spark** the Trust was operating dredgers capable of clearing channels to a depth of 50 feet, with each individual vessel capable of moving half-a-million cubic yards of sand annually. Then – following traditional practice which remained unchanged for nearly a century – the resulting sludge was ferried out to the deeps of the Irish Channel and dumped from self-propelled hopper barges.

In parallel with these improvements the great docks were excavated and the associated quays, warehouses and cranes were constructed. In the way of all things, the wheel has turned full circle and now the vast majority of the docks have been in-filled and the reclaimed land turned to other uses.

But when the humble puffer fleets sailed down stream from the Broomielaw they were the shrimps of the river traffic, plying a waterway and an estuary which had been created to carry international maritime traffic of every conceivable description and dimension – and in huge volume.

It used to be said that the Clyde made Glasgow: in truth, it would be more apposite to say that Glasgow (and above all the Navigation Trust) made the Clyde.

The *Para Handy* stories, written by a man born and raised on the firth, who spent his working life in the inner heart of a city dependent on the river for its prosperity, reflect Munro's own love for and knowledge of the river. And as befits the pattern of life on the Clyde at the time, the pages are rich with references to individual vessels, both real and imaginary, and to categories of ship types which mirror the huge diversity of traffic on and around the estuary – from the humblest puffer to the most richly-caparisoned ocean liner.

All maritime life was well-represented on the Clyde and this was naturally reflected in the account of the daily comings and goings of the **Vital Spark**. Once again Neil

Munro presents us with a time capsule of ships and people, memories and traditions, which were as familiar to his readers some eighty years ago as they now seem remote to our modern world.

* * * * *

Coastal sailing vessels were still relatively commonplace, as has been indicated in the previous chapter. More surprisingly, perhaps, is the fact that not only were significant numbers of ocean-going sailing vessels still trading into the Clyde, but many of the Clyde yards were still building them.

The swashbuckling Hurricane Jack (whose fall from grace and from material prosperity is chronicled in another chapter) had, we are told, originally sailed deepwater in square-riggers.

Indeed, worldwide, there were still thousands of these beautiful vessels in commission at the turn of the century. The steamships would see them off in due course, but for the moment the magnificent anachronisms could earn good money for builders and owners alike (if not for crews) and few of the budding deck officers of the time served their initial apprenticeship in any other type of vessel.

Clyde yards such as the renowned specialists Russell's of Port Glasgow were still launching four-masters into the first decade of this century and all the big-name yards such as Fairfields, Connells, Inglis of Pointhouse, Lithgows, Stephens of Linthouse had an excellent track-record for the design and construction of fast and successful sailing vessels as well as the ever more dominant steamers.

One sailing clipper featured in the stories is at first sight likely to be dismissed as purely fictional, because of the context in which her name is brought in. In the story titled simply *Hurricane Jack [III/1]* we are told that the eponymous subject of the chapter made a passage of just 39 days from Sydney to San Francisco while in command of the clipper **Port Jackson**. The natural assumption is that no such ship ever existed.

In fact, there actually was a ship called **Port Jackson**, a very famous four-masted iron barque of 2,100 tons, built by Hall's of Aberdeen in 1882, and described in Basil Lubbock's classic volume *The Colonial Clippers* as ".....always considered one of the most beautiful iron ships ever built."

And, yes, she did make passage from Sydney to San Francisco in just 39 days, her best 24-hour run a staggering 345 miles, and she was only three days slower than the mail steamer on the same crossing.

Like so many fine ships which had, somehow, succeeded in taking on the steam power which was coming to dominate the seas and survived into this century, she was a war casualty, torpedoed by a German submarine in 1917.

Square-riggers and schooners in fact played a prominent role in the First War, and not only as cargo carriers in circumstances which dictated that all the available shipping tonnage of every description had (necessarily for the survival of an island people) to be pressed into service.

They were even numbered among the ingenious Q-Ships – those decoy "merchantmen", in reality naval-crewed vessels, whose role was to lure unsuspecting submarines to the surface, and to their destruction. This ruse is discussed later. (See Chapter 6: *The Vital Spark and the War.*) The unlikely incarnation of the puffer as one in a series of tales which are clearly intended by Neil Munro to be seen as the product of Para Handy's imagination is the only example of deliberate self-parody encountered anywhere in the stories.) But though the majority of the real vessels which played the demanding part of "wolves-in-sheep's-clothing" were in fact steamships, some of the Q-ships were sailing vessels: and very successful some of them were, too.

The other side of that particular coin – and an astonishing one it is – concerns the Clyde-built clipper

Pass of Balmaha, which was launched from the renowned Port Glasgow yard of Robert Duncan in 1888.

After a distinguished and occasionally record-breaking series of passages in a quarter of a century of commercial trafficking she was captured by a U-Boat while sailing under the American flag of neutrality and taken by a prize crew into the German naval base at Cuxhaven.

Here the Germans turned a Scottish-built windjammer into a supposedly Norwegian ship which would deploy a conscious and deliberate reversal of the British Q-Ship ruse! Where those vessels' objective was to lure the unsuspecting submarines to the surface, the Germans' equally deceptive transformation of the **Pass of Balmaha** was intended to tempt a British prize crew to board an innocent-looking "neutral" – whereupon they were seized and the sailing vessel's hidden guns uncovered and trained on their own ship.

The late Basil Lubbock, in his superb series of monographs on the last of the great sailing ships, suggests that the wiles of the **See-Adler (Sea Eagle)**, as the **Pass of Balmaha** was renamed by the Germans, were deployed successfully no fewer than fifteen times before she herself was stranded and lost on a Pacific Island reef in 1917.

The First War achieved nothing other than tragic waste of human life and resources, but marked the sounding of the last trumpet for the world's sailing fleets. Steam had proved irresistible with (relative) reliability and controllability, and increased engine efficiency was delivering power, and speed, at costs against which even the freedom of wind could not compete.

Yet the determination and kindly quirkiness of a handful of eccentric shipowners managed to keep a few of the majestic vessels at work commercially until the outbreak of the Second World War – and attempted to retain a presence at sea even after the war, though that gallant effort lasted for just a year or two.

It's doubtful if even Para, optimist though he was, could have foreseen that the beautiful ships on which his hero Hurricane Jack had sailed – as skipper, no less – could have survived for another generation and a half. Certainly MacPhail would never have believed it possible!

The doyen of these shipowners was the Finn, Gustav Erikson, operating out of the Baltic Åaland Islands whose people – and entrepreneurs – were wholly devoted to the traditions and the values of the sea. Åaland owners had more than 200 sailing vesels criss-crossing the oceans of the world before the First War and it was Åaland owners, headed by Erikson, who bought up much of the sailing tonnage which had survived that war. From Erikson's tiny home port of Mariehamn his great ships sailed out to carry Australian grain round the Horn to Europe till 1939. He still had a fleet of 17 square-riggers at sea in 1933 though by then there were, apart from his ships, only four other windjammers in the world still carrying cargo for a living.

Astonishingly too, it was an Erikson square-rigger which became the first maritime casualty of the Second World War. She was the **Olivebank**, a four-masted barque of 3,000 tons gross, built on the Clyde by Mackie & Thomson in 1892, originally for Weir's famous "Bank" Line. Returning to her Baltic base in September 1939 after a voyage from Australia, she sailed into a German minefield off the Danish coast, blew up and sank.

Only four of Erikson's ships survived the Second War and in 1957 his barque **Pamir** – ironically sailing under the German flag by then, with a cargo of Brazilian grain – was sunk by an Atlantic hurricane while on passage from South America to London. That was a historic tragedy, for she was the last sailing vessel ever to carry a cargo for commercial gain.

Just a few years previously, one more Clyde link with the great sailing ships – apart from those few like the **Cutty Sark** at Greenwich, and the **Balclutha** at San Francisco which have been preserved (hopefully) for all time – had been severed when the Clyde-built barque **Archibald Russell**, also an Erikson ship, was sent to the breaker's yard.

Still making the Cape Horn passage to the Pacific as late as the 1920's and 1930's, she had been launched at Scotts yard, Greenock, in 1905. She was the very last four-masted barque built on the Clyde and could perhaps have been a familiar sight, as her hull took shape against the low green Renfrewshire hills, to the crew of the humbler **Vital Spark** as she chugged her painful way slowly up the river on a dreich winter afternoon with a cargo of Loch Fyne timber and an indiscreetly belching smokestack.

* * * * *

As well as different classes of ships of all types, Neil Munro brings "on stage" many vessels by name. Some are pure fiction but many are real ships, and again their variety is eloquent testimony to the panorama of sail and steam which was set out on the Clyde Estuary, taken so much for granted, and seen as an immutable part of an unchanging way of life on the river.

Throughout history the Clyde has been a vital naval resource both in peace and in war. The recent withdrawal of the United States Navy from their Holy Loch base is just the latest in a long line of on-off relationships between the Clyde Estuary and the navies of the United Kingdom and its allies.

Neil Munro could never have foreseen how the anchorages at Tail o' the Bank and the Gareloch would become assembly points for the enormous convoys of the Second War, but he was very aware of the Clyde's significance as a naval asset in the First War, and the uses to which it was put then and in earlier years. Hence the frequent allusions to naval events and vessels.

The oldest vessel named – which admittedly has no association with the Firth! – is the 100-gun first-rate battleship **Royal George**, built in 1746 and later the flagship of Admirals Anson, Howe and Rodney. She makes an unlikely cameo appearance in *An Ocean Tragedy,* episode 16 of the third collection. This is the splendid story of how Para Handy, having brought the **Vital Spark** to port in the teeth of a fierce gale, gets so carried away with his account of it to fellow travellers on the train to Glasgow – fellow travellers with a generous and freely circulating bottle, needless to say – that by the time he gets home he has come to believe himself that the puffer is sunk.

"By the time the consolatory bottle was finished", writes Neil Munro, "the loss of the **Vital Spark** had assumed the importance of the **Royal George**."

The fate of that vessel was that, while she lay in harbour at Portsmouth in August 1782 crowded with peddlers and hawkers, as well as with the womenfolk of much of her crew – wives or otherwise, the Navy of eighteenth century Britain made no moral enquiries and set down no moral judgements – she was canted over for repairs to her strakes and copper sheathing and water flooded in at her lower gunports. She could not be righted quickly enough, and keeled right over and sank with the loss of almost 900 lives.

Two things strike home about the use of the **Royal George** as the touchstone for this story.

First is the certainty that at that time the name of the ship and the circumstances of her loss must have been familiar to Munro's *Evening News* readers: otherwise, he would have chosen some other example. Yet today, who has ever heard of the **Royal George** and her fate?

Second, it is significant that Neil Munro did not cite the recent loss of the **Titanic** as the historical parallel in this story: since that tragedy had taken place only a few years beforehand, he would have felt that any casual reference to it in a humorous story would have been seen as being in the worst possible taste.

From a distant perspective, we can look back on the tragedy of the White Star liner with relative equanimity: eighty years ago, presumably, Neil Munro's public would have the same neutrality of feeling in connection with the story of the loss of the English first-rate ship-of-the-line.

In *Piracy in the Kyles [II/15]* we come across the obsolete battleship **Collingwood**, laid up in the Kyles. The sheltered anchorages in the sea lochs around Bute are still used today as parking places for ships which nobody has a use for: vessels – both naval and merchant marine – about to be scrapped, or made redundant by a glut of tonnage and a slump in demand for their services. Loch Striven and Loch Ridden, as well as being two of the most beautiful sea lochs in Scotland, suffer by virtue of being easy of access from the Firth so that ships can readily be moved in and out of them. Since they are very remote, at any rate by road, from major population centres, there are likely to be few complaints from the public at large when they are thus used as maritime refuse tips.

To be fair, though, the problem is nothing nowadays to what it was in earlier years. At the time of writing only one derelict "super-tanker" is littering the matchless beauty of Loch Striven.

The pace of the advances in naval architecture has always been rapid – in Neil Munro's days as well as in our own. When Para Handy comes across the **Collingwood** "mothballed" in the Clyde in 1902 she was just 15 years old.

She was built at Pembroke Dockyard and commissioned in 1887, a 9,500 ton vessel with a crew of 500. She spent most of her active service on the Mediterranean station before being consigned to limbo on the Clyde, and she was finally broken up in 1903.

When the **Vital Spark** encounters her on passage from Tarbert on Loch Fyne, two fishermen are scraping mussels for bait from the lower plates of the rusting hull.

Para Handy views the operation with some contempt.

"They're a different cless of men aboot the Kyles from what there used to be," he remarks: "or it wouldn't only be bait they were liftin' off a boat like that. If she wass there when Hurricane Jeck wass in his prime, he would have the very canons off her."

An observation which, of course, leads into a story.....

The next naval vessel to be brought into the tales is the battleship **Formidable**, but only in an aside, in reference to the fact Para Handy's friend Colin Kerr is serving on her.

She was a 16,000 tonner, built at the Portsmouth Dockyard and commissioned in 1901. At the time at which Munro refers to her she would have been with the Mediterranean fleet. It's to be hoped that young Kerr moved on: the ship was torpedoed by an Italian submarine on New Year's Day, 1915.

"**Hood**, ahoy!" was one of the insults flung at the **Vital Spark** towards the end of her career from unfeeling passengers on the decks of the turbine greyhounds which sped past the puffer and left her astern as if she were lying at anchor.

There had been an earlier ship of that name, an undistinguished pre-Dreadnought battleship of 14,000 tons, the navy's last turret ship and the last to have the unusual configuration of twin funnels placed abeam: commissioned in 1895, she was scrapped before the outbreak of World War One.

Thus there is no doubt that the vessel with which **Para Handy**'s pride and joy was so unfavourably compared was the Clyde-built **HMS Hood**, launched at John Brown's Govan yard in 1918, just a matter of weeks before the end of the First War.

She was commissioned two years later as the largest, the most powerful and – at 32 knots – by far the fastest battleship in the Royal Navy. The country in general, and the Clydesiders in particular, who had built her – or watched her building – held her in pride and esteem.

Her early years, when Para Handy and his crew would have come across her, were a time of triumph for the new darling of the navy. Her end was a national tragedy played out in the darkest days of the Second War.

By 1939 she had been overtaken by the new technologies of naval architecture and naval warfare, but she was still serving – by necessity as well as choice – in the front line of maritime defence in the United Kingdom. She was therefore a key player in the squadron dispatched into the North Atlantic to intercept the German battleship **Bismarck** when, in May 1941, that ship broke out of the Norwegian fjord in which she had been lying.

The two ships were much of a size in terms of dimensions and tonnage. There, however, the similarity ended. **Bismarck**, just a year old, represented the latest in state-of-the-art naval technology and the manifestation of raw power. **Hood** was twenty years older, outdated and at the very end of her useful life. Her speed – her one remaining "plus" – had only been made possible by making reductions in the weight, and therefore the effectiveness, of the protective armour-plating on her hull.

The two warships encountered each other for the first and last time in the Denmark Straight, lying between Iceland and Greenland, on the morning of May 24, 1941. The German's first salvo bracketed the British battlecruiser and one "lucky" shell penetrated her armour and exploded in the main magazines with catastrophic effect.

HMS Hood, the perceived public epitome of British maritime strength, blew up, disintegrating, and sank in moments. Out of a complement of 1,169 officers and men, only three survived. It was a naval disaster without precedent.

* * * * *

The two super-liners which find their way into the narrative were both Clyde-built for the Cunard Line: yet they could not have had more dissimilar careers, one ending her life in the tragedy of a brutal act of aggression in wartime, the other passing out her time in a wash of public esteem and affection.

The four-stackers **Lusitania** and **Aquitania** were both built at John Brown's Clydebank yard.

Lusitania was the first British liner to have four funnels. The configuration was not absolutely necessary, but there was a tendency for transatlantic passengers to make their own private assessments of the prestige of the vessels competing for their custom, and the number of funnels mounted was seen as having some bearing on the status of the ship which carried them! This was a trend which foreshadowed the twenties, when Union Castle festooned the (relatively speaking) diminutive **Arundel Castle** and her sister ship the **Windsor Castle** with four funnels when, as a later conversion proved, two were more than enough and aesthetically far more pleasing: and the thirties, when even the revered **Normandie**, thought by many to be the most beautiful steamship ever built, was given a third, dummy funnel which housed little more than the kennels for her passengers' pampered pets.

Lusitania was launched in 1906 and sailed on her maiden voyage the following year. She was 760 feet overall, and displaced 30,000 tons. On May 7, 1915 she was engaged on her normal business – at least insofar as any sort of normality was possible in wartime. She had not been requisitioned by the Government for military duties, but was on passage from New York to Liverpool with a civilian crew and civilian passengers.

In the early afternoon she was steaming off the southern Irish Coast in the vicinity of the Old Head of Kinsale. At 2.10 she was struck just for'ard of amidships by a torpedo fired, without any warning, from the German submarine U-20. In just 18 minutes she was gone, and 1,201 men, women and children perished within sight of land.

The **Aquitania** in contrast had a long and relatively uneventful career, despite the fact that she was requisitioned as a troop carrier in both World Wars. She was significantly larger than the **Lusitania**, though with a superficially similar four-funnel silhouette. Going into service in 1914, she was 900 feet in length, displacing 45,000 tons. In a career which spanned almost forty years she became firmly established as the "grand old lady" of the North Atlantic crossing. Her final passage brought her back to the river in which she had been created, to the breaker's yards at Faslane on the Gareloch in 1950.

Crowds lined the firth to watch her last homecoming – including myself, then a ship-crazy schoolboy.

It would be totally trite to say that we shall never see her like again: but she deserves to be remembered with pride.

Many of us have memories of the **Aquitania** if only as a glorious vision sweeping across a distant sea and skyline.

Para and his crew saw her too. To them she was one out of a whole fleet of liners, albeit one of the grandest of them, carrying out duties which – they must have thought – would be as unchanging as time itself. She was the epitome of the transatlantic lifeline. Passengers and freight went by sea, or they did not go at all. To those of us who were lucky enough to see her she was a time-shift taking us back to those confident days.

Since her passing, there have been two further generations of passenger-carrying vessels many of which, at least till the sixties, came from the once-great yards of the Clyde. It is probably simply regret for days which are irrevocably lost that prompts the feeling that these two further generations have seen a steady retreat from the character and standing which marked their progenitors.

The "middle" generation, launched from the thirties to the early fifties, were the great **Queens** and their contemporaries, providing services worldwide that were half trans-ocean lifeline and half leisure cruises offering the literal lap of luxury. But at least they were still liners in the great tradition, and provided a scheduled service, albeit it one in decline, which criss-crossed the oceans.

Now we have the "today" generation: the floating gin palaces of modern legend, whose resemblance to a real ship is purely coincidental, whose raison d'être is to cosset the paying guest in surroundings which are deliberately designed to ensure that any similarity to sea-going fact is smothered by pampered and land-based fiction. The scheduled sea-routes have been destroyed by air-transport and sea travel today is a luxury, not a necessity: its patrons tourists rather than travellers.

At the beginning of this century, however, both the ocean-going liners and the estuary minnows shared one common heritage. They provided an essential transportation link to the people and the businesses in the communities they served.

Sadly, today, that vital element of mutual dependence which integrated transportation supplier and transportation customer has – with the welcome exception of the island communities and a scattering of the remoter peninsulas – been largely usurped by road, rail, and air communications.

By their very nature, such means of conveying people and things tends to be either very personal – in other words, carried out with your own car in situations where you meet nobody else at all: or very impersonal – as in a plane or train, where communication between the provider of the service and the user is virtually non-existent.

Only on the essential ferry services – the few left in the islands, the fewer left on the Clyde – does the spirit of the days of the **Vital Spark** live on.

And as for international communication, the days when the Clyde was one of the cross-roads of freight and passenger traffic worldwide passed away years ago. Nowadays the plastic airlines serving plastic food to plastic people going on plastic holidays have stolen the character which was once the hallmark of travel – any sort of travel – and which certainly made the Clyde and everything it stood for a power to be reckoned with – socially, culturally and economically – at both local and international levels.

Underpinning all the banality of late twentieth century society, the river and its memories can sound a tangible and sadly missed echo of the days when people mattered more than things, and when how you travelled and with whom was probably more important than where to, and certainly more significant than how fast.

CHAPTER 4

The Puffers

It is not easy to define just exactly what it was that gave the puffers their special magic but make no mistake, a special magic they did indeed have. Nothing else explains the affection attaching to them.

They were not creations of beauty. They had about as much charisma, as much delicacy of appearance and litheness of movement, as a floating bathtub. Their sea-going qualities were notoriously bad, their engines under-powered and their crew's accommodation basic in the extreme.

Their calling was not romantic. It was humdrum. Worse, there were times when it was downright demeaning. They carried filthy cargoes in foul weather, frequently either to remote roadsteads where the crews had to do their own stevedoring, or to squalid jetties specially designated for puffer traffic and hidden in a shamefaced nook of an otherwise steamer-smart harbour, like the stool in a corner on which the schoolboy in disgrace was sent to do his penance.

There was little kudos for those who manned them. They were all too often treated like second-class citizens by the officers and crews of the river steamers and sea-going ships, and certainly sneered at by the socially ambitious yacht owners and their professional crews.

They did not make serious money – at least certainly not for the crews. And many of the skippers who scrimped and saved to buy their own command found out that the economies of scale were tipped in favour of the big owners, that there was no way in which they could compete against the fleets of John Hay, or Ross and Marshall: especially when these dominant forces not only ran fleets, but even built and maintained their boats in their own yards as well.

The work involved in their day-to-day existence was at times downright dangerous, often back-breaking, usually involving long unbroken hours, always without benefit of union or employee protection.

There was a monotony about the daily routine for many of the little boats. Perhaps they carried identical cargoes to the same ports year in and year out. Perhaps – worse, far worse – they were engaged in coaling the Atlantic liners which lay off Greenock embarking their emigrant passengers, week after unchanging week, or perpetually carrying what seems to have been the most hated bulk cargo of all (on account of its pungent, penetrating, irritant dust) – limestone.

Yet for all these and other shortcomings the puffers have come to occupy a very special place in the affections of almost everyone who knew them and, perhaps more remarkably still, that affection is not based merely on nostalgia. People do quite genuinely miss the little boats. Many other long-discarded objects of an earlier generation – trams, for instance – are only remembered with affection retrospectively. In their time the trams were usually cursed as slow, noisy boneshakers which were a major factor in traffic congestion. Puffers, on the other hand, seem to have been regarded with much the same affection when they were still around as they enjoy today. They did not have to wait for their passing to give them sentimental status and nurture a sense of regret at their demise. Even ninety years ago, when Para Handy first came to life in the old *Glasgow Evening News,* there must have been public esteem for the little boats: otherwise the stories could not have run and run, as they did, for twenty years.

Perhaps more surprising still is that people who

have never in their lives so much as seen a puffer can respond to their appeal just as much as those who were familiar with them to a greater or lesser degree. Just how else can one explain why the Para Handy stories have rarely, if ever, been "out of print" for sixty years, or how BBC Television's periodic re-creations of them attract huge audiences and sell thousands upon thousands of video tapes of past programmes?

The final enigma is that, yes, the real-life crews appear to have had just as much blind devotion to their unreliable, uncomfortable and un-prepossessing craft as did Para Handy himself. It is a happy revelation to talk to the men who once skippered, engineered and crewed the little boats and see how much intense pleasure they take in reliving memories of their days on board: how their eyes light up even when they are relating tales of monotony, or of hard work, or of the threat of danger: how their infectious enthusiasm for that long-vanished way of life spills over into everything they have to say.

Perhaps the small scale of the boats, their crews and their way of life has something to do with it. Puffers were intensely personal craft. So was the service they offered, the means by which it was delivered, the human element always to the fore in a way which it could never be in the larger scale of serious shipping business.

Of the source of at least one particular and persistent myth about the puffers there can be no doubt. Neil Munro, in creating Para Handy and vesting the **Vital Spark** with a totally uncompromising Glasgow base, must surely be responsible for the entrenched belief that they were a type of vessel peculiar to the Clyde and the west coast ports. That is one myth now so firmly locked into the national sub-conscious that it is surely impossible that it should ever be overturned!

While it is true that there were more puffers on the Clyde than on any other stretch of coastal water and that (because of the topography of the estuary) they had what the marketing men of today would term a "high profile" —

in plain English they were almost constantly in sight –
they were not a product solely of this river. Puffers carried
cargoes to and from east coast ports, at least as far north
as Aberdeen, at least as far south as Tyneside. Kincar-
dineshire barley loaded at Stonehaven for shipment via
the Forth and Clyde Canal to the distilleries of Campbeltown or Islay was quite a usual contract.

Moreover, the puffers actually started life as canal
craft designed specifically for use on the Forth and Clyde
link. By far the biggest fleet in existence was that operated
by John Hay & Co. In their near century of successful
operation they owned more than ninety of the little boats
and deployed them from Kirkintilloch, an inland town
straddling the canal some twenty miles from its Clyde
origins at Bowling! Even worse – or at least even stranger!
– is that very few of the puffers were actually built on the
Clyde. Hay's had their own shipyard, at Kirkintilloch of
course. McGregor's yard, another which specialised in
building puffers, was also located there. In Glasgow itself,
at Maryhill, Swan's boatyard launched generations of
puffers. Others were built on the Monklands Canal. Some
slid down launchways in Northern Ireland. And most
difficult of all for the aficionados of the exclusively Clyde
puffer myth to accept, all but two of the sixty or so final
generation of puffers – the so-called "**VIC**" boats – were
built in yards in England!

Do all these facts destroy the entrenched public
perception of the little boats as being exclusively "Clyde"
puffers? Is the notion a total misconception?

Well, not really. Wherever they were built, most of
the little craft did indeed serve out much of their lives on
the estuary and in the harbours of the Highlands and the
Western Islands. There was a large element of truth in
what became a not wholly accurate myth. The boats were
usually Glasgow registered: they were usually manned by
West of Scotland crews. It's just that they did go farther
afield than is often realised: moreover, precisely because
they were such a successful type of craft, they did encour-

age the establishment of one or two puffer colonies in "foreign pairts": and they really started life as canal-based craft (which limited their size to an overall length and a laden draught which the locks could accommodate).

* * * * *

Those very first puffers were built on the Forth and Clyde canal, and were intended to operate on it. They carried Baltic timber west from the docks and seasoning basins of Grangemouth, coal and iron ore east to the foundries at Carron. Their size was limited by the 70 ft. locks of the canal: the first puffers were all about 66 ft. in length, with a crew of three, and a cargo capacity in the region of 100 tons. They had no form of bridge or wheelhouse, but were steered by tiller. Their original hull form was based very much on that of the sailing gabbart which they replaced.

As traffic increased and the demand grew for versatile inshore craft which could operate to remote communities independent of piers and harbours the puffers moved out of the canal and traded to a wider market, making the original sailing coasters redundant as they did so. By Neil Munro's time they had evolved into a size and configuration which would change little over the last sixty years or so of their useful working life.

There were two basic types of puffer operating at the turn of the century. The smaller, which conformed to that original 66 ft. length which had been dictated by the canal lock sizes, carried a crew of just three – skipper, engineer, deckhand. They were known as Estuary boats and were restricted to the sheltered waters of the firth. They were not allowed to operate beyond a line from Garrioch Head on the south east of Bute to the lighthouse on the island of Little Cumbrae. However, they could trade to the Loch Fyne ports provided they took passage there by way of the Kyles of Bute.

The sea-going boats, to which class the **Vital Spark** belonged, reached a maximum length of around 80 to 85 feet. Few of those built prior to the outbreak of the Second War, however, were of that greater size: most still conformed to the classic 66 ft. dimension but were constructed to a specification which allowed them to operate outwith the Garrioch Head restriction zone. They carried a crew of four – skipper, engineer, mate and deckhand. They could operate where and when they pleased with no restrictions. Such puffers became the cargo-carrying lifeline of the Western Highlands and Islands and without them many of the remotest communities could not have survived. They also shipped cargoes regularly to and from Northern Ireland and, as noted above, there were others providing a regular freight service up and down the east coast as well.

Eventually, towards the close of the puffer era, some of the largest puffers – the ex-Ministry of Defence **VIC** boats for instance – had a crew of five and the skipper, who on the earlier puffers shared the cramped fo'c'sle with the crew, had a tiny cabin to himself beneath the wheelhouse. On the real "de-luxe" versions, so did the engineer.

The **VIC** boats were a wartime creation. Of the original design more than sixty were built – all but two in English yards. The term **VIC** was an acronym for Victualling Inshore Craft and they served as supply tenders to assembling convoys, to warships, to invasion fleets in almost every theatre of war. There is probably no greater accolade for the concept of the original puffers than that in a time of national emergency, when any resources would have been made available to provide the best possible answer to any given problem, the considered opinion was that in providing an inshore cargo carrier capable of going almost anywhere and doing almost anything, the humble puffer was an ideal blueprint which could not be improved on.

The Ministry went on to build a second series of **VIC**s but these were slab-sided for the sake of speedier construction and the resemblance to the original puffers was marginal. Of the first series of **VIC**s, however, many which survived the war years were bought from the Ministry by private shipowners and a number were in service in the West of Scotland till the very last days of the puffers.

Indeed, two – **VIC 32** (with wartime economy of imagination the little craft were simply given numbers instead of names and she has retained hers) based at Crinan, and the renamed **Auld Reekie**, based on the Caledonian Canal – have thankfully been saved and, converted, are still sailing – as "cruise" vessels for summer visitors.

And one, the very last of her line, still earns her living as the **Vital Spark** did almost a century ago, tramping mixed cargoes and bulk freight to the remotest communities and the farthest corners of the West.

As an aside, it should be pointed out that the puffers were actually "puffers" for only the first few years of their hundred year history. The earliest boats were so named because their steam engines were not fitted with condensers but vented their exhaust gases directly into the funnel: the result was a distinctive "puff-puff-puff" sound.

That first nickname stuck. Within a few years, condensers were fitted and though the distinctive sound disappeared, the little craft's by-name did not. It even stayed with them to the very end, although by that time the last surviving puffers had been diesel-engined for years!

* * * * *

Life on board would have been no bed of roses. Spells of really intense activity in harbour, particularly when the crew had to do their own loading and unloading in the absence of dockside facilities and even dockers themselves, would have been a sharp contrast to the sheer boredom of long sea passages which, at the puffers' top speed of around seven knots, must have seemed interminable. Indeed, puffers were frequently reduced to a virtual standstill if they were trying to make progress against a brisk headwind when carrying a hampering deck-cargo such as timber. Confidence and courage were other attributes which most puffer crews must have had in abundance. It was one thing to chug full-laden along the Forth and Clyde Canal with a freeboard measured, quite literally, in inches rather than feet. It would have been a very different proposition taking a bulk cargo of, say, granite chips to Stornoway given the stormy reputation of the Minch and the puffer's total inability to run for shelter if the need arose.

The carrying capacity was around 100 tons for the typical coal-fired puffer, but the saving in space and deadweight following conversion to oil-fired engines hiked this figure by 30% and that fact, coupled with soaring costs of coal after the Second War, and the labour-intensive way in which it was supplied and used, encouraged fleet owners to convert to oil power as quickly as possible.

Puffers carried anything, anywhere. That was their strength. No harbour? Puffers could be beached to transfer their cargoes on the ebb into waiting carts or lorries – or vice versa. No cranes? The simple mainmast derrick could be adapted (with the appropriate accessory) to discharge or take aboard goods or bulk material of any description. No dockers? Puffer crews loaded and unloaded their own vessels as a matter of course.

The usual cargoes for the run-of-the-mill contract would be materials in bulk. Barley from the grain-growing flatlands of Angus and Kincardine to the distilleries at Campbeltown or Islay. Timber from the forestry plantations beside the clachans and hamlets of Lochs Long, Goil and Fyne. Sand from the Holy Loch. Granite from Furnace. Fertiliser. Coal. Bricks. Cement. Whinstone. Limestone. Even whisky in bulk from Campbeltown, or Islay, amid ingenious speculation about how that particular cargo might be "tapped" and a little of the product "liberated"!

Puffers carried other things as well, of course.

Groceries and hardware to the remoter island communities. Livestock for the annual sales at Oban or Portree. Flittings. Machinery. Motor vehicles.

Puffers did other things, sometimes more interesting things. In wartime they supplied the assembling convoys at the Tail o' the Bank and serviced the naval vessels which patrolled the estuary and the islands. A thriving black – or at least grey – market attached to that particular line of duty! In peacetime they ferried food and drink, fuel and fitments to the west coast lighthouses, both on and off shore, for the Commissioners of Northern Lights.

For a century they were the workhorses of the canals and the upper reaches of the river: but they were at the same time versatile thoroughbreds uniquely able to provide the service which kept the remoter Highlands and Island communities alive.

Those who depended on them trusted them: those who saw them as they went about their business looked on them with affection.

Those who served on them, loved them.

CHAPTER 5

The Puffer Men

Ian McColl was born in 1911 and brought up on the banks of the Crinan Canal, and lives now in Glasgow, last of his generation of a family of one girl – and 10 boys. His father was lock and bridge keeper at Cairnbaan, half way between the eastern and western termini of the Canal.

Of the 10 boys, one died in infancy: but most of the others, almost without exception, finished up at sea for life, in one shape or form.

Alasdair, for instance, was on the puffers and during the Second War crewed a **VIC** which was strafed by a German plane in Rosyth Harbour. "You could see daylight through her funnel where the bullets had hit home" says Ian.

Brother Neil went deep sea, then came home to join the police for some years before signing on again. Donald was on the puffers all his life, an accomplished and experienced skipper: so – though in the engine room – was Cecil, "the one in the family wi' the posh name".

Findlay was on MacBrayne's paddler **Mountaineer**, on the service between Crinan and Oban. He was berthed there the night the handsome **Grenadier** went on fire in 1927 and he was among the rescuers who managed to pull all but three of the crew of the doomed ship to safety. He was regarded as "the best heaver of a line in the whole MacBrayne fleet." Twice Findlay fell into the docks himself on the way home from a spree: twice he was rescued. He couldn't swim a stroke, says Ian, but then none of them could, excepting only Neil.

Willie was in puffers but decided to emigrate to America. He was like the **Vital Spark**'s Dan Macphail, says Ian: he was far happier with a book in the fo'c'sle than spending his evenings in the pub with the rest of the crew. He eventually got fed up with his shipmates constantly coming back aboard the worse for wear, and packed it in.

Donald was "a legend" says Ian. He lived in Greenock – so did Cecil – and had been on the puffers from the age of 15. He worked for several years for a Greenock owner called MacNeil who was nicknamed "The Haddie" (though nobody seemed to know why) on the **Auburn** and **Ardfern**, and for many other fleets as well. Donald was a "very daring man". He would need to have been for he was also a very unlucky one. He was on the **Moonlight** when her boiler exploded and she went down off Ardnamurchan, the Larne-built **Jenny** when she went ashore in bad weather on Eigg in 1954, the **Lady Isle** when she was wrecked at Scarinish, Tiree in 1956.

Once he reached skipper status Donald McColl was namely, as Para might have phrased it, for taking puffers through the Crinan single-handed if their crews failed to turn up in the morning after a night before at Ardrishaig or Tarbert. He did exactly the same thing but as a matter of regular routine during the last war, when he was skipper of a puffer on duty victualling the convoys assembling off the Tail o' the Bank. On those occasions he would claim for three men's wages, and get away with it.

Whereas Cecil, the engineer, was a "whisky" man, Donald was a beer drinker. Ian says that the Greenock police used to help Donald safely home if he'd been on a spree, even to the extent of seeing him across the road and up the close, for he was the man who kept them well supplied with otherwise hard-to-come-by titbits during the war – little treats sneaked ashore from those victualling excursions.

One Hogmanay in the 1950s, it was whispered, Donald arrived home late and well-watered, but desperately in need of something to eat in an age when the late-night take-away was an undreamt-of paradise. Fearful of waking his sleeping wife he prepared a sandwich snack in the darkened kitchen and in the morning an empty tin of catfood was lying beside the bread-bin. "It was damn'd good at that," said Donald when his wife berated him.

Donald was born with that instinct which distinguishes the sailor from the ordinary mortal. He had an unfailing "nose" for the weather. Ian recalls sailing with him on one occasion when he hauled the crew from their bunks at 1.00 a.m. while the boat was berthed at East Loch Tarbert on an autumn night of peace and dead calm. They would leave for the Kyles and Glasgow that instant and no argument about it. They did. An hour after they reached the shelter of the upper river one of the worst storms of the decade hit the Clyde and confined puffers – and larger vessels too – to harbour for near a week.

Cecil, says Ian, had a "great sense of fun: a few halves on board and he'd start an argument with anybody and about anything. But he was a gentle soul with it." He was also, like Macphail, a realist in the matter of a puffer's engine and its abilities. Many times he would be trying to bring one round the Mull against wind and tide and, however much coal he threw into the furnace, she would just stand still – holding her own but making no headway whatsoever.

Ian himself values memories of a gentler, happier world on the Firth which has gone for good.

When they were children he and his brothers used to race MacBrayne's little passenger boat **Linnet** along the banks of the Crinan Canal from Cairnbaan to Ardrishaig while the travellers and excursionists on board threw pennies for them to catch, to divert them and slow them down.

Ian McColl worked for many years in the office of an engineering company in Glasgow till the late forties, when his brother Donald persuaded him to put up the money ("I was no wealthy man, but I never smoked or took a dram, and I had a bit saved.") to buy a puffer for himself. Donald would be the skipper and the engineer was Jimmy Macmillan from Islay. Ian was "chief cook. bottle-washer and dogsbody".

The boat was a little three-man estuary boat, the **Craigielea**, which was bought, for about £1,000, from the Dewars of Rothesay. She had been built – Ian can't remember when, but thinks it would probably have been about 1900 – at Dumbarton.

Ian looks on the years that followed as the happiest of his life as the "family puffer" fought off all the attempts of the well established fleets to squeeze them out of business. Competition was keen, and none too scrupulous at times.

Ian was contracted to do a lot of work for Millar the builders, transporting bricks, timber and other materials to development sites at Rothesay and Millport. They would come up the Forth and Clyde canal as far as the docks at Maryhill, load up, and return to the river. This involved them in negotiating ten locks on each leg of the canal journey. Bowling basin was the point at which the puffers left the canal for the Firth, and their movements there were always dictated by the tides.

"We would always wait for the ebb before we left the basin, so as to get the current with us on the way downstream. The same heading back: you used the tides in a puffer, you never tried to fight them unless you had absolutely no choice. She just didn't have the power." On the way back from Bute or Cumbrae "light" they would sometimes put into the Holy Loch and beach her at Sandbank, loading a cargo of sand with their own winch and bucket-dredge, and come right up river to Stockwell Bridge right in the centre of Glasgow to unload – a process which involved having to lower the mast to get under the intervening bridges.

Though like all estuary boats they were restricted to the inner Firth, in bad weather "it could be pandemonium: many's the bad fright I got, but Donald was a wonderful,

wonderful sailor and he saw us through." Ian remembers vividly one night when they came out of the Holy Loch, which is a well-sheltered anchorage in most winds, with a full load of sand and were hit by an unlooked-for gale of wind which swept the overladen puffer broadside down towards Dunoon totally out of control and nearly put her on to the Gantocks rocks – a reef which has been the end of many a larger ship – before they were able to turn her head to the wind and get just enough way on her to steer her away from trouble.

There was another occasion when he was chartered to bring up to Gourock a huge tractor-shovel from the farm on Inchmarnock Island, Bute. To load the beast they had to beach the puffer and winch it on board. This was not a major problem as the boat was keel-grounded and sat steady despite the enormous weight of the machine out to starboard as they craned her up and over the side. It was a different matter at Gourock, where they berthed to unload their cargo actually at the main steamer pier. "There was a crowd there bigger than a Partick Thistle football match," Ian recalls, "desperate keen to see what was going to happen."

What happened, of course, was that the moment the tractor was swung up out of the hold and outboard over the pier, it very nearly tipped the little puffer (her hull now light and riding high in the water) on her beam ends.

"Donald yelled at us on the winch to drop it, and by God we did that good and fast, or it'd have had us over."

On the way up and down river they would often overnight in the East India Dock at Greenock. With a tiny crew and lacking even the most basic navigational aids, puffers rarely sailed after dark if they could avoid it. Tragically it was in taking that safety measure that Ian lost the **Craigielea**. One night in 1950, when he was living in Greenock, they berthed the puffer in the harbour and went home for the night. He was wakened in the small hours by the police with the news that the puffer had been crushed on to the dock wall by an incoming boat laden with a cargo of granite chips from the Furnace quarries on Loch Fyne, sprung her plates, and sunk.

The particular poignancy of the disaster was that the engineer on the incoming puffer – one of the Greenock-based Ross and Marshall fleet – was Ian's brother Cecil.

"For all the years after that Cecil would say he just couldn't understand how it had happened, they'd just brushed the side of the wee boat, they couldn't have broken the shell of an egg."

But that was the end of the **Craigielea** and of Ian's flirtation with the chancy business of puffer ownership. There were few one-boat owners. Most of the puffers were in the fleets and the largest of these was Hay's, followed by Ross and Marshall.

* * * * *

Duncan McColl, Ian's nephew, Neil's son, sailed with Ross and Marshall in the early fifties on that company's five-man boat **Sealight**. Built by Brown of Greenock in 1930 she was a seagoing 85 ft. boat with a carrying capacity 30 per cent greater than the little estuary vessels. She was one of the Rolls-Royces of the puffer world. Although she was still coal-fired (she would convert to oil later that decade) she had proper "heads" – a luxury unknown on the little Craigielea where, Ian said "You waited till you got where you were going if you possibly could" and her skipper had a tiny cabin to himself under the wheelhouse. Later and even larger Ross and Marshall boats had all the accommodation aft, with a separate cabin for the engineer as well.

Sealight's voyaging took Duncan much farther afield. They went through the Crinan and then the Caledonian canals as far as Inverness to pick up a cargo of electricity poles for the island of Tiree. They took coal to Portree on Skye and on the return voyage loaded up with timber from Raasay island. On that particular voyage Duncan's skipper took a sadistic delight in pointing out the rusting remains of the **Jenny** on the rocks off Eigg with the remark that "Your Uncle Donald put that one there!"

Bigger she may have been, but life on the **Sealight** was no sinecure and Duncan remembers some unnerving trips. One of the problems of the puffer-class was the lack of freeboard when full laden which meant that even modest seas could sweep their decks from end to end. Another was that if she was carrying a bulky but "light" cargo such as timber, she would ride high with little "grip" in the water and was tossed hither and thither like a cork. If the timber also included an element of deck cargo the situation was made even worse.

A third disadvantage of the puffer was her very limited speed which meant that she could never "run" for shelter, but only crawl: and similarly if the weather was to worsen seriously in mid-passage, en route to Ireland perhaps, there was nothing she could do but press on.

Duncan's two worst memories both involve cargoes or planned cargoes of limestone, the bête-noir of most of the crews on account of its noxious and penetrating dust.

On the first occasion they were bound from Bruichladdich in Islay to the little port of Glenarm in County Antrim which served a limestone quarry. **Sealight** was running light, having discharged a cargo of coals at Bruichladdich, when she was hit by sudden and excessively violent winds which in no time had created horrendous seas. This was one of the relatively rare night passages and for Duncan it was about the longest night of his life as the little boat, with no cargo to offer any sort of stability, was given a tremendous battering.

Even worse, though, was the abortive passage from Oban to Tobermory full-laden with a limestone cargo and a ponderous and bulky deck-cargo of a lime spreader and additional machinery as well. Their progress against a rising westerly was painfully slow and as the storm grew in ferocity the well-deck was often knee-deep in water. Then the real nightmare – the deck-cargo began to shift. **Sealight** was in distinct danger and, despite the risks attendant on turning broadside to the incoming seas, she was turned around and crawled back down the Sound of Mull and eventually found shelter in the lee of Kerrera where she lay till the storm passed. It was Duncan's worst experience ever and one in which even the puffer's veteran skipper was "white about the gills."

Another unforgettable passage was the one on which they spent nearly a week in vain attempts to get round the Mull of Kintyre on the way back to Glasgow with a cargo of timber from Raasay. Fortunately this was not a trip fraught with danger and looking back on it, Duncan laughs at the memory. They could not get back to the estuary by the usual Crinan route as the Canal was closed due to repairs being carried out somewhere in the locks system, so they had to take the long way round via the Mull. There was a strong, though not threatening, head wind and with her huge deck cargo catching it full on, the wretched puffer could make almost no seaway against it! The force of the wind was quite simply exceeding the power of her engine to counter it and they had to turn back on four successive days to overnight at Craighouse on Jura, or the Crinan basin itself!

Duncan was deckhand and cook when he first joined the puffers and was responsible not just for preparing the food, but for provisioning the boat in the first place. Wages were about £9 a week at the time and the crew had to provide their own "kitchen" which meant a levy on each man of about 30/- (£1.50) per week. Lorne sausage – the square blocks of sausage meat still on the market today – was a popular staple, and there was always a barrel of salt-herring in the fo'c'sle in case they were ever stranded or running short of fresh supplies. Duncan's reputation as a cook was founded on his ability to provide good steamed puddings ("that filled them up") and that was certainly a luxury which neither The Tar nor Sunny Jim offered on the **Vital Spark**.

Quite a bit of provisioning was achieved by the barter system of which the owners were unaware – though probably they had their suspicions. Coal was the commodity. Going through the canals, Duncan recalls, buckets of coal were traded with the houses and farms for eggs and milk, butter, fruit and vegetables, bread. In Campbeltown Loch, they sailed towards the harbour through a fleet of fishing vessels. "I was on the hatch of the hold like a goalkeeper, catching the fish bring thrown to us from all sides." Later that evening, when the fishing boats returned to port, they were repaid: with coal.

Indeed on some boats it was not unknown for the puffer to "inadvertently" slip forward in the loading dock as coal was being chuted into the hold so that a goodly proportion of the contents of the chute finished up in the ship's own bunkers. As Para Handy found out, you could get around the harbours at little cost if your cargo was coal..... It was also not unknown for the unsuspecting consignee to be offered a "little extra" out of the puffer's bunkers when she arrived at her destination "at half price". This was of course his own coal, for which he'd already paid full price!

Duncan had great admiration for his first skipper, Willie Sutherland. A fine seaman "but he was like Para Handy too. I'd had visions of sitting round yarning, but Willie was aye on at you to work on the boat, get out the paintpot or the tarbrush."

An occasion when Willie was off sick and a "relief" skipper was in charge brings memories of rather less happy times and Duncan recalls being left on board as watchman when she was berthed at Campbeltown while the rest went ashore – and came back much the worse for wear.

Despite the usual aversion to night-time sailing the skipper decided to head for home forthwith – but just half an hour out from Campbeltown he came down to rouse his sleeping deckhand and order him to take the helm.

"I was alone at the wheel all the way to Gourock, six or seven hours or so, with no experience and always worrying about the lights and other shipping. Mind you, it was a beautiful night and I'll never forget the thrill of it in retrospect but at the time I was scared stiff."

For Duncan, that was enough hassle – and he stayed "ashore" till his regular skipper was back!

* * * * * * * *

The estuary puffers made trips of just a day or two: the larger boats such as **Sealight** could be on trips which took up to a week, though if these ran into one another they could be at sea for longer than that.

Occasionally, though, there were contracts which by their very nature meant that just the one "job" could stretch into weeks.

Eoin McArthur made one such trip shortly after the last war on the **Lady Isle** – the very same puffer which later wrecked on Tiree when Donald McColl was skipper. She was owned when Eoin sailed on her by Duncan McCorquodale who was originally from Lismore but now lived and operated his business in Troon.

The puffer was chartered by an Ayrshire coal merchant for the unusual and attractive job of taking in the year's coal supply to three of the west coast lighthouses. Eoin had been in the merchant marine before the war and had served in the Royal Navy during the war, losing a leg at the successful Allied landings at the mouth of the Scheldt, and was biding his time before embarking on a civilian and land-based career.

The two week trip round the lighthouses, in the most beautiful summer weather, was a tonic on which he looks back with much pleasure. It was also, however, a great deal of hard work.

They had to unload 25 tons of coal at each of three lighthouses, and at the island of Lismore, and all the work fell to the crew. The lighthouses serviced were Ruadh nan Gall on Mull, just north-west of Tobermory, Eilean Musdile off the south point of Lismore and Fladda Island, to the west of Luing.

The bunkering of the lighthouses was a nightmare task. At both Ruadh nan Gall and Fladda the puffer had to lie off, and the coal had to be bagged and slung into the ship's boat to be rowed ashore in "loads" of just three or four bags at a time. At Eilean Musdile the puffer was able to sling the cargo ashore on to the island's tiny, makeshift "jetty" (hacked out of the natural rock) using the ship's derrick: but it had then to be manhandled to the light-keepers' houses – by the puffer's crew.

Only at Lismore Island was there some relief, when the boat was beached and the tonnage destined for the island homes swung into waiting horses and carts which came out at low tide to load up in turn.

On the way home the puffer passed through the Crinan Canal late in the afternoon and, though there was no chance of a daylight passage home to Troon, Eoin remembers that the skipper was hoping to get to Lochranza at least (on the north west corner of Arran) or maybe even Brodick itself, before a last short run the following morning. The younger crew members were less than happy about this as they discovered at Ardrishaig that this was the evening of the annual Tarbert Fair and they would gladly have put in there overnight.......

They did so in an episode that could have been taken straight from the pages of the exploits of the **Vital Spark**!

"The engineer – literally – put a spanner in the works," Eoin recalls. "The skipper was hopping mad, he knew just what was going on but when the engineer says he needs to put in for repairs you can't argue.

"It really served us right that as soon as we had berthed the heavens opened and it poured for the whole evening and the rest of the night!"

The **Lady Isle**'s skipper-owner was a real link with the Clyde of days gone by: Duncan McCorquodale had served his time with MacBrayne's, like so many other puffer men. But in his case his berth had been on the venerable **Glencoe**, a paddler from a far generation, originally launched and named the **Mary Jane** in 1857 which was in continuous service till she went to the breakers nearly three quarters of a century later in 1931!

* * * * *

Ross and Marshall was a Greenock company, founded in 1872 and in their time they were shipbuilders as well as shipowners. It is as the operators of the famous fleet of puffers, all of whose names ended in the suffix "lite" or "light" that they are best remembered. The last owners of the company were apparently very anxious to achieve the centenary of the business. They failed by just two years.

Eighty five year-old Donald Clarke has now moved on to enjoy retirement in South Africa but he served on the **Mellite** in the 1930s. She was a purpose-built puffer of quite unique characteristics. Her function was to be luggage tender and, above all, water carrier to the armada of passenger liners which were then shuttling in and out of the Tail o' the Bank anchorages to and from the American ports, north and south. She was therefore not a cargo-carrier with a hold, but a mini "tanker". Her tanks were filled not with oil fuel but with fresh water which she took out to the waiting liners. She returned with their passengers' luggage as the owners of it were being deposited on the pier at Greenock, usually by paddle steamer.

Through the winter the **Mellite** was also on contract to maintain and repair the moorings of the yachts in the Holy Loch and the other centres such as Cardwell Bay in those pre-marina years.

It was maybe a predictable routine but it was one remembered by Donald with much affection for the camaraderie and spirit of the Clyde, and with much gratitude for the fact that he had a job at all in the darkest days of the depression. "10/- (50p) a day all found!" he recalls: "I was rich!"

Donald went on to a long and successful career at sea which included a spell as chief engineer on the Iraqi royal yacht but in common with so many of his colleagues it's his time on the puffers that he looks back on with the greatest nostalgia.

Twenty years later, the marine superintendent of the Ross and Marshall fleet from 1956 to 1970 (the year a take-over saw the death of the company's hopes of centenary celebrations) was Glasgow-born George Anderson.

A seafarer all his life George was previously in the merchant marine in the thirties and during the war, and served seasons as chief engineer on almost every one of the remaining "rump" of the classic Clyde steamer fleet in the early fifties.

Nothing that happened in, on and around even the most reprobate or scallywag Clyde puffer could ever faze a man who reported to take up post as second engineer on a wartime cargo vessel, the **Templeyard**, at Hoboken, New York, to be greeted with the news that she was ready to sail, she'd just completed loading – with 4,000 tons of artillery ammunition!

"They wouldn't let us join the convoy," he recalls: "We sailed some miles astern of it and each evening one of the escorts would double back to see if we were still there." To make matters even more precarious they had a boiler breakdown and were reduced to half power for two days: but in the end made it safely to Port Said – via the Cape of Good Hope, since such a valuable consignment for the desert war couldn't be risked in the killing grounds of the Malta channels!

After the war he stayed on in the merchant marine, plying to Australia and the Far East, but in 1950 decided that home was best and settled in Glasgow, taking up a chief engineer's billet on the Clyde fleet. He served on them all, from the venerable **Duchess of Fife** to the pioneering **King Edward**, then in her last season before going to the breaker's yard, and the newly innovative diesel-electric paddler **Talisman** which had been launched just before the war.

When George joined the company in 1956 they had nine puffers, ranging from the smaller three-man estuary boats right up to the biggest of them all, the five-man

Stormlight: they still had Donald Clarke's old charge the **Mellite** as well, though the need for her was fast disappearing as the liners abandoned the Clyde, the passengers abandoned the liners, and the burgeoning airlines hijacked the transatlantic traffic.

The company's "commercial" office in Glasgow dealt with the administration of the vessels, and secured their cargoes. Down at Greenock George Anderson's responsibilities were keeping the little boats at sea: maintaining and overhauling engines, machinery, hull. Scott's Yard in Greenock had the contract for the ongoing upkeep of the fleet: R & M's own shipyard, which had built many puffers as well as maintained them, had closed in the 1920s.

The Superintendent's life was not an easy one. The boats, quite astonishingly, had no radio communication. Skippers with a problem had to put in somewhere to find a telephone and they would call George at any hour of the day or night: so would families needing to get messages to crew members. Skippers out in the islands or Western Highlands also had to phone Glasgow, once their cargoes were discharged, to ask "Where to now, and for what?" They would also phone Glasgow if conditions were bad and they were going to be delayed. Being a commercial office, says George, Glasgow were not particularly tuned in to the realities of weather. "What d'you mean the weather's too bad for the boat to put out," went one typical exchange with a skipper somewhere in the Hebrides: "What are you talking about? It's a beautiful afternoon here!"

The crews were characters to be admired. The skippers didn't have certificates – just experience: the engineers were not qualified: they were just tackle-most-things handymen. The deckhands were grafters. They came from all over the Highlands and Islands as well as from the Clyde. To many of them, the single men, the wee boats were the only home they knew.

"Puffers just couldn't work nowadays," says George.

"For a start, overtime would see to that. Above all, they meant a way of life that the 1990s just would never accept. Away from home for weeks on end and without any sort of schedule to be able to give families an idea of when they would be home. At least the deep sea ships do run to some sort of a timetable."

The uncertainty of the puffers' movements is something that is rarely thought of. Some boats – especially the estuary puffers like Ian McColl's **Craigielea** – tended to be out one day and back the next. But the seagoing boats could be off to Raasay with coal, then to Mull to pick up timber for delivery to Islay, to Furnace for granite for Oban: and so it could go on.

There were magic moments. George was called out to Girvan one afternoon in the sixties to a Ross and Marshall puffer chartered to the BBC for the filming of a television series of Para Handy. The engineer reported on the phone that he couldn't get water into the boiler. When George arrived, he discovered that the engineer had accidentally but carelessly stood on a vital valve-cock, turning it the wrong way, and so the water was pumping overside instead. He tore him off a thorough strip in the engine-room and climbed on deck: to be greeted by the actors Roddy MacMillan (Para Handy) and John Grieve (Dan Macphail) saying "Thank the Lord we're not crewing under you!"

And tragic ones. The much larger Ross and Marshall coaster **Polar Light** left Liverpool in heavy weather and foundered at sea: only one man survived.

There were near misses. One of the 'lights' was blown ashore on Raasay after her engine broke down and they couldn't refloat her. George Anderson went north to oversee salvage operations and they finally managed to break the "vacuum" that was sucking her into the sand by digging under the hull so that the incoming tide could get beneath her and release her.

A dram came into the equation, of course. There was the skipper who sent his 'hand' ashore for supplies and when he came back with bacon and eggs, two loaves, and two bottles of Scotch greeted the man with "What in blazes did ye buy a' that breid for?"

Taking barley to the Islay distilleries was a popular contract in those days for it was traditional for the crew to be given a generous dram of "white" whisky when the unloading began and again when it finished. And of course the skipper could always find some reason for needing to visit the distillery manager in his office.......

There were some nice apocryphal tales too. Or were they? It was said that one puffer arrived at Islay to load a cargo of whisky in bulk, in the barrel. The distillery trucked the precious cargo to the pier, barricaded and padlocked the gate of it, and posted security men on watch on the pier itself overnight. Some clever characters crept under the pier, along the horizontal trusses, manoeuvred an augur between two of the deck-timbers of the pier itself and bored a hole into the base of one of the barrels at the centre of the stack. Needless to say they had an adequate supply of buckets and barrels of their own waiting to capture the golden flood........

* * * * *

The Ross and Marshall fleet was the last serious, versatile puffer fleet in business. They were able to handle contracts as diverse and skilled as the laying of underwater telegraph and telephone cables in addition to their more routine work. Their crews, as George Anderson testifies, were like the crews of any puffer – resilient, courageous, hard-working and, though they might have been the last to admit it, God-fearing in the way of all men who seek a living in a dangerous environment.

From one of them he "collected" this adaptation of the 23rd Psalm which the man had written himself in the 1930s. It seems a very fitting epitaph to a lost way of life.

"The Lord's my pilot: all is well:
His presence brings heart's ease,

The Puffer Men

As I on stormy oceans sail
Or through calm, unknown seas.

"My soul he doth restore again
And me to sail doth make
On every course that he commands
E'en for his own name's sake.

"Yea, though I round the cape of death
Yet will I fear no ill:
For thou art with me and thy love
So great gives comfort still.

"With thee at table richly spread
In face of deadly foes,
My mind with truth thou dost illume
And my heart overflows.

"Goodness and mercy all my life
Shall surely sail with me,
And when the Port of Heav'n I reach
I'll go ashore with thee."

There always had to be a more committed attitude to the whole business of crewing a puffer than met the eye. For surely few occupations could put a man more at the mercy of the elements, or make him more aware of his dependence on the skill and the courage of his fellows: and on the protection of some greater force as well.

Fact Meets
Fiction

—

CHAPTER 6

The Vital Spark and the War

The war that changed the world for ever was a watershed for the Clyde as well. What in 1914 had seemed a settled and unchanging social and economic way of life had by 1919 been overturned for ever. On the west coast, as everywhere else in Europe, halcyon ignorance of the suffering which man could inflict on man had been replaced by the bitter experience of a conflict which had destroyed the established and accepted order and replaced it with a new and uncomfortable hierarchy – locally, nationally and internationally.

That is maybe chief of the reasons why the **Vital Spark** made but a handful of token appearances in the immediate post-war years and then went to the literary breaker's yard, despite the fact that Neil Munro remained a working journalist (by now editor of the *Glasgow Evening News*) until his retirement in 1927. There would be little enthusiasm for re-creating a lost world which was already being looked back on with nostalgic regret for a vanished innocence: equally Para Handy and his crew would have been anachronisms in the new order which was being painfully shaped in the twenties.

* * * * *

As the war ended, the puffers were still plying the firth although some had been on admiralty business, acting as fleet tenders, victualling craft and the like. Most of the Clyde steamers, on the other hand, were far from home – requisitioned for wartime service and now deployed in almost every zone of naval conflict. Others, lost in the course of their war duties, would never return to the Clyde.

The **Neptune**, which ran the Greenock, Rothesay and Kyles of Bute service up till 1914, became a mine-sweeper based at Dover. She blew up in the English Channel in 1917.

Minerva was another paddler from the Rothesay run: stationed at Malta as an naval auxiliary she was captured by a Turkish frigate while on patrol among the Greek islands. On conclusion of the armistice, the Turkish Government paid compensation for her and retained her as an Istanbul ferry.

The unfortunate **Mars** was engaged for mine-sweeping duties in the North Sea but was run down and sunk by one of our own destroyers off Harwich.

The first **Duchess of Montrose** was just as unfortunate: she was sunk by a mine while sweeping off the Belgian coast. Later, a much-admired turbine steamer bearing the same name came from Denny's Dumbarton yard in 1930 and maintained the summer service to Inveraray into the 1960s.

The first **Duchess of Hamilton**, precursor of the fine turbine steamer of the same name launched in 1932 for the Campbeltown service, was used as a transport vessel in the North Sea. She struck a mine and sank in 1915. Though the second **Hamilton** was built at Harland and Wolff's Govan yard, she bore a quite uncanny resemblance to the Denny yard's second **Montrose** and the two vessels, virtually sister-ships, were almost impossible to tell apart at any distance.

Other Clyde vessels were more fortunate, getting away with no worse than a narrow escape. **Mercury** twice struck mines while on sweeping duties, blowing off first her bow and then her stern but she was repaired on each occasion, returned to the Clyde at the end of the war, and lasted a further 14 seasons.

Some went far afield on active service. The **Queen**

Empress came under enemy fire and ran aground in the White Sea en route to Archangel. She was successfully refloated. Also on convoy duties to that northern Russian port (as an ambulance vessel) was the pioneer **King Edward**. The former Clyde paddler **Marchioness of Bute** had been sold to East Coast owners in 1908 and during the war she spent some time actually stationed at Archangel on mine-sweeping duties. A similar input to the war effort was made by the **Marchioness of Lorne**, first in central Mediterranean waters based at Valetta, latterly in the Levant theatre, operating out of Port Said.

Some achieved unexpected distinctions. **Queen Alexandra**, more familiar in her later guise (with the addition of a third, dummy funnel) as the **St Columba** on MacBrayne's Ardrishaig service into the sixties, rammed and sank a U-boat in the English Channel. The **Duchess of Rothesay** towed into Margate the damaged hulk of a German Zeppelin airship which had ditched in the North Sea. She survived as part of the Clyde fleet till 1946 and served in the Second War too, taking part in the evacuation of the British Expeditionary Force from Dunkirk. The **Duchess of Argyll** came to the rescue of another Clyde paddler when she towed the damaged **Queen Empress** (see the previous paragraph: she was certainly unlucky in her wartime service) into the port of Boulogne after she had been in collision with a British destroyer.

The paddlers which survived the war were returned to their owners in very mixed condition. Some had been given wartime "additions" such as the reinforcement and actual extension of their bow-plating which had improved their seagoing capability but done nothing for their trim, speed or appearance. Others had suffered so much accidental or casual damage that major refurbishment was necessary. At least one – the **Glen Rosa** – was adjudged not worth repairing, and therefore she was sold for scrap in 1919.

* * * * *

The Vital Spark and the War

Much of the third collection of Para Handy stories
– *Hurricane Jack of the Vital Spark* – were written and set
during the war and this is also the case with the most of the
new tales in the Birlinn Edition. They treat of contemporary issues which would have been talking points, and
indeed in many cases points for argument or complaint, in
a rapidly changing world.

There were government controls on licensing laws,
licensing hours, the quality and strength of the very beer
purveyed, in those "sensitive" areas of the country whose
activities were deemed crucial to the war effort. Needless
to say the Clyde was included among them and it also goes
without saying that these restrictions were not much to the
liking of the crew of the **Vital Spark**. They involved
among other things the sale of ale with a lower proof level
and a curb on "treating": the theory behind that was that
if a man could only buy his own drink, and not stand his
hand, the consumption of alcohol would be less and thus
the danger of over-indulgence affecting work performance and industrial output would be minimised.

The Land Girls whom the crew met in upper Loch
Fyne were another product of the war effort, and indica-
tive of the very radical changes about to burst upon
society. Florence Nightingale, at the time of the Crimean
War two generations previously, had successfully pioneered the concept of women performing a caring function in wartime, nursing the casualties of the conflict back
to health. Now for the first time in history women were to
play a major active part in actually helping their country
to win a war. The situation which the country was in meant
that they were needed – but in any case the women
themselves insisted on playing their part.

The campaign for Women's Suffrage had become
an issue of major controversy and confrontation during
the Edwardian years but now the leaders of that movement
swept their adherents into the war effort in their hundreds
of thousands. For years women had worked – often in the
most appalling conditions during the Victorian era – in

menial and poorly-rewarded jobs as a matter of economic necessity, just to help to keep a roof over their family's head. This, though, was different. With the menfolk on active service in their millions, the women became a vital element in the production of the staples of war, and the provision of its infrastructure and services. And because so many men were with the forces, the women were able to seize the opportunity for more rewarding and more responsible employment.

Certainly women worked on the land or in the forestry industry like those whom the crew of the **Vital Spark** met. But they worked in far greater numbers in the munitions factories, the armaments works, on the assembly lines of the fledgling aircraft industry. They drove ambulances and supply vehicles not just throughout this country, but in the hinterlands of the Western Front. At the end of the war a grateful government rewarded them – though only stage by stage – with the voting rights for which they had fruitlessly campaigned for so many decades. Indeed some historians suggest that the extension of suffrage was the country's way of thanking the women for their unstinting contribution to the winning of the war, and that they would otherwise have waited decades more before universal suffrage was as much their right as that of their menfolk.

Para Handy's crew also came up against the new-fangled Daylight Saving Act *(Summer Time on the Vital Spark [III/18])* which was introduced by Lloyd George's Government in 1916. Advancing the clocks one hour ahead of the standard Greenwich Mean Time gave more daylight at the end of the working day and the purpose of the exercise was twofold: partly to extend the useful working day – but above all to cut electricity consumption. Almost all power at that time was provided by coal-fired stations and any reduction in consumption in that area increased significantly the tonnage of coal which could be devoted to the needs of the war. Para Handy ranted against the notion of "tamperin' wi' the time o' day the way God made it" but so great were the advantages of the system that "British Summer Time" became part of our way of life and in the Second War, there was even Double Summer Time, with the clocks advanced two hours on Standard Time.

Wartime shortages were a fact of life and it was inevitable that some hint of them would affect the **Vital Spark** and so appear in print in the stories.

Eggs were either too plentiful and used *ad nauseam* for the lack of tastier fare *(Eggs Uncontrolled [III/19])* or in short supply in the cities, offering the opportunity for a little judicious grey-marketeering by the crew *(Para Handy in the Egg Trade [BP/96])* with eggs from Mull. The shortage of beer has already been touched on: the shortage of butter encouraged Hurricane Jack to "acquire" a goat – which unfortunately for his plans turned out to be a billy! *(A Rowdy Visitor [III/8])* Food of any description would have been welcome in the case of Dougie's grimly unsuccessful *Foraging for the Vital Spark [BP/93]* but every effort is made to see that the men in the front line at least are well-provided for in *The Canister King [BP/89]*.

Though the real "black market" never reached quite the heights in the First War that it scaled in the Second, it did exist and so did all other kinds of profiteering and racketeering. The nearest that Para Handy and his crew came to encountering the rackets that were being set up was just before the outbreak of the War when they came across the devious Englishman Mr Denovan in the Greenock public house. *(Confidence [II/24])*. He was masquerading as an Admiralty agent, in Scotland "to arrange for housin' the torpedo workers". This was a reference to the munitions factory under construction at Cardwell Bay on the boundary between Greenock and Gourock. The factory was still going strong during the Second War: today, the site is occupied by a cash-and-carry warehouse.

It was also shortly before the actual outbreak of war *(The Stowaway [II/23])* that the crew are panicked into believing that a Basque onion-seller found hiding in the fo'c'sle is a German spy.

In some of the stories set during the War, the **Vital Spark** is sailing as a three-man boat, Sunny Jim having managed to enlist in the army by masquerading as Dan Macphail after his first attempt failed when the examining M.O. discovered that he had a glass eye. The last thing Macphail wanted, in contrast to Jim, was to be conscripted and the engineer was more than happy to swap identities *(How Jim Joined the Army [III/22])* when he was called for examination and, to his horror, drafted. Dan had been "practising" to fail his medical and neither he, nor Para Handy, could understand how things had gone wrong.

"'Did you no cough at them?' asked Para Handy. 'Yon chrechling cough wass chust a masterpiece.'

"'Cough!' exclaimed Macphail. 'I coughed till ye would think it was the Cloch on a foggy night, but yon chaps never heeded.'"

* * * * *

The most intriguing of the wartime stories, however, have to be those in which the **Vital Spark** is portrayed as a "Mystery Ship" or "Q-Boat". There are four of these and they link together to form a continuous narrative: *The Mystery Ship, Under Sealed Orders, A Search for Salvage* and *The Wonderful Cheese* – numbers two to five of the third series.

They are a unique quartet. All the other tales in the Para Handy repertoire, whether narrated by the skipper himself or by Neil Munro as the onlooking author, are plainly fictional but are presented – within the ground rules of fiction – as if they are fact. In other words, if we could step through the looking glass into Para Handy's world, then they could all have really "happened". But not these four. Para Handy has made them up, he has created his own fictional stories within what is already a fictional world.

They also happen to be four of the best of all the tales, spun by the skipper to a group of Glasgow holidaymakers and telling of the wartime exploits of the puffer as a Mystery Ship with Hurricane Jack in command. In the course of the stories, he succeeds in sinking a U-Boat and is awarded the V.C.

It is slightly surprising to realise that the secrets of the Mystery Ships and the full details of precisely how they operated were in the public domain so quickly after their first devising. The most famous factual account of them – *My Mystery Ships* by Rear-Admiral Gordon Campbell, V.C. – was not in fact published till 1928, and ran to many editions in the years that followed.

Put simply, a Mystery Ship was a commandeered merchant vessel crewed by naval personnel. To all outward appearances she was an unarmed, unprotected and tempting target for any enemy submarines. In fact, she had had naval guns installed aboard her but hidden from view behind sham bulwarks or inside a fake deckhouse.

Torpedos were extremely expensive weapons and furthermore there was a limit to the number which the U-boats of the period were able to carry. Once her torpedos had all been used up, the cruising U-Boat had lost her effectiveness as an attacking force capable of capitalising on her fighting power no matter the circumstances and situation of the opportunities presented, and she had to return to base to replenish her weaponry. This was wasteful of time and also of course reduced the number of U-Boats on patrol.

Therefore it became normal practice in the early days of the war for a U-Boat encountering a lone and unprotected merchant ship to surface, give the crew a few minutes to abandon ship, then close in and sink her by gunfire This was a cost-effective means of despatching the vessel, and also one which conserved the submarine's stock of torpedos so that these were available for use in circumstances where a surface attack was out of the question, such as at night, or in targeting ships in convoy or under escort. It was to take advantage of this tactic that the Mystery Ships of the First War were created.

A submarine surfacing to sink one of them by gunfire would in normal practice put a shot across her bows and order the crew to abandon ship. This would appear to happen as a well-schooled "merchant marine" crew took to the lifeboat, though of course the real crew, hidden beside the ship's guns, remained on board. The submarine would then, hopefully, move in towards her target, since at close range she could be sunk with minimum use of ammunition. When he was convinced that the U-Boat was as close to the Mystery Ship as she was likely to come, the naval commander on board would give the signal, the white ensign would be run up the mast, the shuttering hiding the guns dropped away, and the gun crews would open fire on the submarine, hoping to inflict mortal damage on her before she could make an emergency crash-dive.

The Mystery Ships were not an invention of the First World War, however. Campbell, in the opening chapter of his book, traces their origin way back to the days of sail with the first recorded deception of this type taking place during the reign of Charles II when an English naval captain "housed his guns, showing no colours, striking even his flagstaff, and working his ship with much apparent awkwardness" to lure an enemy privateer to her destruction during the Dutch Wars. There are accounts of similar ruses being employed during the naval wars with France in the time of Nelson, and Campbell quotes at length from the anonymous letter published in the *Naval Chronicle* of 1811 which gives a very detailed proposal for the deployment of what would have been really quite sophisticated forerunners of the decoy ships of a century later.

The unknown writer proposed using "merchant vessels having as little as possible the appearance of ships of war each having on board such a number of men as may be considered....well trained to the use of the musket and rifle" to cruise offshore as bait for privateers so that "when attacked by the enemy under a conviction of them being private vessels, our men (who might easily keep themselves in concealment till this period) might without difficulty give them such a lesson..."

Basically, then, there was nothing totally original about the Mystery Ships of the First War in terms of what they were trying to achieve, and how. There were two big differences however. The first was the deployment of what was known as the "panic party", the purported civilian crew who deserted the decoy vessel at first sight of the submarine. The second was the size, power and nature of their quarry and the unnerving strength of its armaments.

Initially the Mystery Ships enjoyed a very encouraging success rate with three sinkings in their first two months. The problem though was that the secret of their use, and methods, could not be kept secret for long. As the war at sea progressed U-Boat captains became understandably paranoid about lone merchantmen and it became increasingly difficult to lure them to the surface. Despite the costs involved, torpedos soon became the order of the day in most circumstances. Even when a U-Boat did surface, it was usually to circle the merchantman at a considerable range and try to finish her off without having to come close by – no matter how long that might take. In the last action which Campbell commanded, the Mystery Ship **Dunraven** was spotted by a U-Boat which stalked, circled, and inspected her through periscope when submerged, binoculars when surfaced, for *five* hours: shelled her at intervals, wounding many of the hidden gunners on board: and finally torpedoed her. At no time did she come within what Campbell considered a "useful" range, so the British ship never had a chance to open up her guns but instead the men had to lie doggo, under scrutiny and under periodic fire, for five solid hours.

In all, the Mystery Ships sank just 11 submarines, representing 7 per cent of the total number of U-Boats lost to allied naval action during the war. But they damaged about 70 more and, perhaps most important of all, they had a shocking effect on the morale of the German crews. As Campbell said with probably deliberate understatement: "One can easily imagine that it must be a bit of a shock to be lying off a harmless-looking tramp or sailing-ship and suddenly find you are up against a man-of-war bristling with guns." A shock, indeed!

It will be realised from the reference to sailing-ships in that extract that though the Clyde puffers, in spite of the vivid imagination of Para Handy, may not have been deployed as Mystery Ships, sailing vessels certainly were – and with some success too.

* * * * *

As the First War came to an end then so, but for a last dying flicker, did the life and times of Neil Munro's puffer and her crew, at least in the fictional guise of the **Vital Spark**. The real puffers, however, would continue to ply the Clyde and the Western Islands for a further half-a-century and make many more friends in the process. The undiminished popularity of Munro's stories has ensured that, long after the last skipper of the last puffer is nothing but a distant memory, the tales about the little boats and the men who crewed them will live on to amuse and entertain generations to come.

CHAPTER 7

The Demon Drink

The fact that generalisations are usually inaccurate and sometimes downright dangerous has never stopped people from making them: so here goes.

Sailors reputedly have a weakness for the bottle: Scotsmen at large and Highlanders in particular are credited with a certain fondness for a dram. The likelihood of these assertions proving to be true, we are told, can with all confidence be doubled in spades if those against whom they are being made fall into the terrible-twin sub-category of being both seamen and islanders. They say that ports such as Stornoway or Portree are the only places on earth where you can actually see people being carried *into* a pub.

It's no surprise therefore that the **Vital Spark** could scarcely be described as a teetotal boat. Indeed, the crew's somewhat relaxed attitude towards the demon drink is established once and for all in the very first story.

Advanced a one pound note (a very useful sum round which to construct a party in those days) for ship's expenses, they are well and truly led off the straight and narrow. On this occasion, unusually, the man responsible is Dougie the mate, who is more often cast as a follower rather than as a leader. But it is at his behest that Para Handy and the crew head for the snug bar of the nearest hostelry.

Here, as Para Handy relates, Dougie "rang the bell of the public-hoose we were in, and asked for four tacks and a wee hammer. When he got the four tacks and the wee hammer, he nailed the pound note on the door, and said to the man, 'Chust come in with a dram every time we ring the bell till that's done!' "

The result of that particular spree was the – temporary – loss of command for the captain, and of employment for the crew. But they never allowed the experience to deter them, and a fondness for a dram leads them into many a scrape in the stories which follow.

There rarely seems to have been any drink actually carried on board the **Vital Spark**, though. In *The Malingerer [1/3]*, before it's realised that the Tar is merely feigning illness to get out of loading a cargo of timber, there is a suggestion that Para keeps a "medicinal" bottle. It is never referred to again. Apart from the gift of a bottle of whisky from a satisfied customer referred to in *Three Dry Days [1/22]* the only time when there is drink on the ship is when the crew go ashore to buy beer and bring it back – usually in a gallon can.

It seems that the crew's reaction to the availability of drink was the same as that in the story of the Argyllshire man who walked every evening three miles there and three miles back, to and from his croft, to get to his nearest inn, no matter the season or the weather. Once there, he downed two quick drams and headed for home.

After some months of this, the innkeeper said: "Wullie, ye'd save yersel' a long trup every nicht, and mony a soakin', if ye were tae come over once a month, buy a couple of bottles and keep them in the hoose."

"Dinna be daft," said the crofter. "Whusky disnae keep!"

It certainly didn't on the **Vital Spark**.

Fortunately both Captain and crew, fond of a dram though they might be, were of a merry disposition rather than a troublesome one when the opportunity to over-indulge arose. The nearest to any drink-induced drama comes in *A Lost Man [1/9]* when Para Handy for some reason falls out with the Tar at the Furnace Ball, gives him a black eye, and sacks him. This incident takes place "off-stage" as it were, with none of the rest of the crew (nor indeed the reader) knowing anything about it. Next morning Para Handy himself has completely forgotten the whole episode and when it is realised that the Tar is not on board, he – and the crew – all presume that he's fallen over the side.

Dougie alternates between periods of observance of the teetotal regime of the Rechabites, and a series of splendid binges. He has something of a reputation in certain harbours of the West. The merchants of Castlebay in Barra, for instance, close their shops when the **Vital Spark** is seen coming over the horizon.

"It needed but the wan or two drams," recalls Para Handy in *A Desperate Character [I/17]*, "and Dougie would start walkin' on his heels to put an end to Castlebay........so when Dougie was in trum for high jeenks, they had a taalk together, and agreed it would be better chust to put up the shutters......

"When Dougie would find the shops shut he would be as vexed as anything, and make for the school. He would go into the school and give the children lectures on music and the curse of drink, with illustrations on the trump. At last they used to shut the school, too, and give the weans a holiday whenever the **Vital Spark** was seen off Castle Kismul. He wass awfu' popular, Dougie, wi' the weans in Castlebay."

Neil Munro uses the local pubs and inns, and their patrons, as a most effective backdrop and setting for much of the action in many of the stories, as a matter of course.

However, while his characters are often marked out for their fondness for a dram – or for the complete opposite, their narrow-minded teetotalism – the crew's frequent excursions to the nearest inn have to be set in proportion.

The local public house, or the "Inns", as it was generally referred to, was in Para Handy's day the hub of village social life. It was just about the only place where men (and they were very much the exclusive province of the male!) could meet and so acted as the fountain and source of news, gossip and business dealings for the community.

In the years before radio, cinema and television, furthermore, the village pub offered the only place of entertainment available, certainly in the remoter communities. It was inevitable, therefore, that the crew of any incoming vessel would at an early stage find themselves heading for the pub.

And a lot more went on there than simply the single-minded consumption of alcohol!

A dram with the local undertaker persuaded him to come down to the puffer to "measure" the Tar for his coffin in *The Malingerer [I/3]:* it was at the Inns at Cairndow that Para hired his tinker piper *[I/14]:* the dispensing of hospitality at the Lochgoilhead farm sale persuaded him to bid for, and buy, a cow *[I/16]:* a temporarily teetotal Para Handy drank a glass of lime juice at the Ferry Inn to the undisguised disgust of Hurricane Jack *[I/22]:* later, in the inn at Bowling, Jack dispensed generous hospitality to persuade Para to accompany him to the Knapdale Ball "to keep an eye on him" *[I/24]:* the confidence tricksters Denovan and Wilson set up their scam in a Greenock public house *[II/24]:* Sunny Jim even bought milk at the Inns at Duror *[III/13]* for many of the rural pubs doubled as the local shop as well.

And so the litany goes on. If there are few of the stories in which a dram does not feature, there are much fewer in which it leads directly to any trouble. However, the reader is left with no doubt about certain facts, albeit not directly connected to the crew of the **Vital Spark**. There was a lot of heavy drinking in certain sectors of the community: and there were occasions when that over-indulgence led to trouble.

Neil Munro does not moralise at any point in the compendium of tales. He is not even consciously reporting on the social condition of the times. He is simply telling stories and it is inevitable that, in the telling, they will mirror some of the shortcomings as well as the strengths of the characters involved.

His attitude to human foibles such as a fondness for a dram is not set out in detail, but rather hinted at by implication, and the suggestion is a kindly tolerance founded on a sense of humour and an awareness of the absurd in human behaviour, rather than a hypocritical condemnation.

A refreshing change in a society in which hypocrisy in such matters was often the order of the day.

* * * * *

Victorian and Edwardian society had an ambivalent attitude to most human weaknesses – none more so than in the case of strong drink.

There is no question that in the cities, heavy drinking was a major social problem in the latter half of last century. There were a hundred reasons for over-indulgence but this little book is not a sociological treatise and won't attempt to work its way through them. For the ordinary working man, though, drink was often an escape route (however temporary) from poverty and poor living conditions. Drink was available and affordable although not quite on the scale of the notorious gin-soaked London of the late eighteenth century when Hogarth's cartoons lampooned the "drunk for a penny, dead drunk for tuppence" drinking dens at their worst and lowest.

Society's ambivalence about the whole drink question showed itself in many ways.

In an age where class had not yet become a dirty word those who regarded themselves as superior, or at least materially better-off, would protest the excesses of those less fortunate in society while stocking cellars of claret, port and brandy for themselves: and making good use of them.

The Directors of the Frith (sic) of Clyde Steam Packet Company Limited (of which more in a moment) could launch the river's first "temperance" steamer: and toast her success in boardroom champagne.

The pubs were shut on the Sabbath except for the refreshment of so-called "bona fide travellers", a non-sense in Scots law which continued into the 1950s. This meant in effect that the thirsty had to travel at least three miles to their neighbouring village or city suburb before they could legally buy a drink. However this legislation did not apply to ships on the Clyde and led unscrupulous businessmen, who might in another manifestation be the first to condemn over-indulgence by the "lower orders", to buy ramshackle second-hand steamers purely in order to run them down river on Sundays as floating shebeens. Sunday boats became so notorious, and so much in danger of tainting all Clyde sailings with the same brush of debauchery and drunkenness, that a group of established ship and steamer owners formed a new company specifi-cally to combat these excesses and restore the good name of the Clyde and its boats as a cruising facility.

This was the Frith of Clyde Steam Packet Company already referred to, and though her board might toast her in champagne, they had had the paddler **Ivanhoe** built by Henderson's yard at Meadowside specifically to be the river's first temperance steamer. She ran as such with considerable success from the summer of 1880 until well into the 1890s: and such was her popularity, particularly with the families which constituted so large a part of the Clyde's regular custom, that her influence was signifi-cant. Other boats did not turn "teetotal": but they did introduce measures which went a long way to control and discipline the sale of liquor on board, and they were helped in considerable measure to redress the reputation of the river when new legislation effectively ended the career of the floating Sunday drinking-dens in 1884.

The whole story of the – typically Victorian – contrast between the temperance lobby at one end of the spectrum and the near bootleggers at the other is very well told in Alan Paterson's books on the Victorian and Edwardian steamers, but the temptation to quote from the press advertisement which appeared to promote the sailings of the teetotal Ivanhoe from Craigendorran pier in July 1882, the time of the Glasgow Fair holidays and the busiest month on the river, is irresistible.

Under the headline "SAFETY AND COMFORT ON BOARD THE IVANHOE DURING THE FAIR HOLIDAYS" the body copy opens:

"As this steamer does not sail to or from Glasgow, Passengers may rely on having a pleasant sail without the *Ordinary Rabble* common on board Clyde Steamers during the Glasgow Fair."

A piece of advertising prose which deserves its place among the most patronising and offensive pieces of publicity ever penned.....

* * * * *

If the battles between the two opposing sides of the drinks lobby had been largely fought out by the time Neil Munro began to chronicle the doings of the **Vital Spark**, Para Handy and his crew had certainly lived through them in the nineties.

What they were still living through, in the period up to the outbreak of the First War, were the death throes of another legacy of Victorian intolerance and hypocrisy – the national temperance movements.

There were local temperance societies a-plenty but the two major players were the Rechabites, which had been founded in the United Kingdom in 1839: and the Good Templars, originally of American foundation and dating from 1852, which crossed the Atlantic some years later in 1869.

Both societies were structured and promoted on vaguely Masonic lines, with talk of lodges and initiation ceremonies, banners and badges and rituals and the rest, but there any similarity ended. For a start, and a most unusual occurrence in the stiflingly patriarchal Victorian social world, women were equally admitted with men. Both organisations recognised that whereas women were rarely themselves burdened with a drink problem, many of them were unfortunate enough to be married to a man who was, a circumstance which would certainly guarantee that they would be doubly dedicated to the promotion of the principles of abstinence and indeed to the very eradication of the demon drink. There was no campaigner for teetotalism quite so ardent as a campaigner who either suffered as a result of the alcohol dependence of another, or who had successfully turned a drinker away from his drink.

Over and above all else, though, the Victorian Temperance movements were a creation of the middle-classes for the lower-classes. There were enthusiastic working-class campaigners to be sure, but the movements were largely characterised by the uneasy mixture of charity and condemnation, carrot and stick, which marked so much of the era's concern for the "deserving" as opposed to the very much undeserving poor.

The campaign for teetotalism seems to have been particularly strong in Scotland: not without reason. Figures of the annual per capita consumption of spirits for 1838 were just under eight pints in England: but twenty eight in Scotland. What is believed to have been the very first temperance movement to be set up anywhere in the United Kingdom began, fittingly enough in all the circumstances, in Glasgow in 1829. It was a first in more ways than one: it predated Victorian "values" by almost a decade, for its middle-class founders aimed to restrict only the consumption of whisky: not the wines and fortified wines, brandies and imported liqueurs, which were their own tipple.

In 1838 the Scottish Temperance Union was founded, with rather less hypocrisy, with the particular motives of providing social alternatives to public houses in the towns and cities (coffee shops) and of encouraging the establishment of an independent network of Temperance Hotels so that neither holidaymakers nor commercial travellers need be tempted from the straight and narrow path of total abstinence.

There were even moves towards copying Scandinavian practices by developing a chain of so-styled "Gothenburg" pubs. In these alcoholic liquor was sold, but the actual opening hours were restricted, customers' behaviour was stringently monitored, and drunkenness or gambling, profanity or lewdness resulted in expulsion and banning from the premises. Sanitised drinking, in other words.

The Independent Order of Rechabites was founded in 1839 and the movement took its name from the teetotal sons of Rechab whose rejection of and abstinence from strong drink is described in the Book of Jeremiah.

It became the mainstream of the temperance movement until the arrival, from America, of the Good Templars whose first Scottish Lodge was founded in 1868 at a meeting of the quite splendidly named "City of Glasgow United Working Men's Total Abstinence Society." Within a year, there were 96. They peaked in the mid seventies with 800 lodges and 62,000 members throughout Scotland, from Shetland to the Borders. But the downward slope was almost as steep: within a decade membership had fallen to under 40,000.

The decline of the movements continued – by the 1890s the Argyllshire Templar Lodges – all 18 of them – could not muster a thousand members, but the Templars fought back with the creation of Juvenile Lodges which insisted on abstinence from tobacco and "profanity" as well as alcohol. Friday evening meetings featured magic lantern slide-shows of the pitfalls of indulgence: the drunkard, the home-wrecker, the criminal, the murderer. Good, cheery and uplifting stuff for the young minds.

An account of the movement, *Good Templary in Scotland,* was published in 1894 and its editorial introduction affirmed total opposition to the "iniquitous drinks traffic" and added that if the book "brings nearer by a day the great and good time when prohibition will be the law of the land, it will not have been published in vain." The history also highlighted some of the notable achievements of the movement: not least among these, as the authors well recognised, was the successful establishment of a Lodge in Campbeltown, the St Kiaran, "one of the most notable in Scotland." Soon 650 members were on the roll, and it was "not unusual for 50 or 60 to be initiated at a single meeting." A notable achievement indeed – in a town with more than twenty distilleries and a population of just 10,000 or so!

* * * * *

Both the Templars and the Rechabites feature in the Para Handy stories on several occasions. Dougie is a backslider of one or other (or indeed both) of the movements, as we learn in *A Desperate Character [I/17]* and Para Handy himself inadvertently joined the Rechabites, albeit for the shortest possible space of time, as chronicled in *Initiation [III/27]*. Elsewhere, Hurricane Jack, in *The Complete Gentleman [II/9]* throws so many empty bottles out of the window of his Caledonian train from Glasgow to Greenock that the line "looked like the mornin' efter a Good Templars' trip."

What is very evident, by the tongue-in-cheek way in which Neil Munro refers to the temperance organisations, is that they have had their day and can have gentle fun poked at them with no great offence. Thus Dougie is very much a renegade in the Rechabites, toeing the line when his wife is on hand to oversee him, but outrageously overstepping the mark when the puffer is safely in distant, Highland waters. Para's brief flirtation with the movement is full of innuendoes from his mentor that the organisation is now something of a gentleman's social and drinking club, rather than the opposite. *[III/27]* "Ye'll find us a lot o' cheery chaps, there's often singing: but ye'll have to come at first deid sober, for they're duvelish particular." And: "Aren't they teetotal?": "Strict – ye canna get over that – to start wi'." Finally, the suggestion that a Good Templar's outing would leave the railway line as littered with empty drink bottles as Hurricane Jack has, shows that the days when the movements were powerful and respected as authorities to be reckoned with have passed. The backsliders, by Edwardian times, are not solely fictional.

Their power-base has been eroded and, to a lesser extent, the need for them has dwindled. But in their day they were both beneficial and influential in a very "mixed-up" society.

* * * * * * * *

Returning to the real world, it's worth noting that the strange juxtaposition of very accessible and relatively inexpensive alcohol to a genuine and widespread groundswell of opposition to the evils of drink, both social and economic, was very typical of the contrasts of Victorian and Edwardian society. A German visitor to Glasgow at the period described it as, paradoxically, at once "the most religious and the most drunken city in Europe."

By the turn of the century, the situation had improved. The excesses of over-indulgence were on the decline and that would continue in the first half of the twentieth century. Arrests for alcohol-related offences in Scotland were almost 50,000 in the year before the outbreak of World War One: exactly a quarter of a century later, the figure was just 17,500.

I think it is fair to say that Neil Munro would not have set so much of the social interaction of the Para Handy tales in the Highland Inns had the drink problem been as serious at the turn of the century as it had been just three decades earlier. But he may have had another reason for allowing the crew of the **Vital Spark** their occasional indulgences. It was suggested earlier in this chapter that one of the reasons for the heavy drinking of the towns of the industrialised central belt was the monotony and poverty of the life which was the lot of so many of their people.

In the times when the local newspaper of an Ayrshire community carried an advertisement praising the qualities of the drink offered for sale by a local public house with the slogan "Drunk for three bawbees, Mortal for three pence" that shrewd and observant commentator, the distinguished geologist Archibald Geikie, was travelling the length and breadth of Scotland in the course of his work. The volume of essays which he produced as a result of his wanderings – *Scottish Reminiscences,* first published in 1904 – is (as well as being at times an extremely funny book) a rare and unbiased appraisal of much of the characteristics, both good and bad, of Scottish society of the period.

Geikie is of the opinion, based on experience, that there was a difference in drinking habits and drinking consequences between the Highlands and the Lowlands: that the Highlander could drink steadily, but hold his liquor: that the Lowlander by contrast drank to oblivion for "a transient escape from the miseries of life, and the only moments of comparative happiness which he ever enjoys".

Thank God that society had come a long way from the terrible indictment which that opinion represents by the time the Para Handy stories were appearing in print, and that the tales could be set in and around public houses, and hint at the occasional problem drinker, without offending and without reflecting a serious social woe.

* * * * *

It seems appropriate that a consideration of the role of the social dram in the Para Handy saga should end on a really low note, as do the tales themselves in that particular respect!

Most of the stories in the third collection *(Hurricane Jack of the Vital Spark)* and most of the additions tracked down for the Birlinn Edition are set during the First World War.

Among the largely forgotten legislation which the Government introduced at the time was a series of measures designed to restrict the consumption (and the effect) of alcohol. If these measures had been applied country-wide they might well have sparked off a revolution! As it was, they were applied in what the government regarded as areas sensitive to the country's war effort and this meant, largely, naval ports and harbours, and the industrial centres which were manufacturing munitions.

Naturally the area of the Firth of Clyde was one of the first victims of the new legislation – legislation which in truth had something about it which was a portent of the conditions created by George Orwell for *Nineteen Eighty Four*. A specially brewed low-alcohol beer – Munitions Ale – was the only beverage available in pubs which were largely state controlled. In some areas indeed – places as diverse as the remote Ross-shire village of Cromarty, adjacent to the crucial Invergordon naval base, and the city of Carlisle, an important centre for armament manufacture – some pubs were taken into state ownership and, incredibly, retained in that ownership till the 1960s! An even worse deprivation was the ban on "treating" – you bought your own drink, and your own drink only. And, needless to say, credit was out of the question.

Para and the crew must have been highly relieved to get away from the restricted upper estuary and out to the more relaxed way of life of the lochside communities. Even here, though, the war could make itself felt – as Hurricane Jack found out *(The Bottle King" [III/14])* when the only spirits available at Peter Grant's remote inns was a bottle of crême de menthe.

Such wartime shortages probably never quite reached in the First War the deprivation of the Second: but they would have been hard to bear for the crew of the "smertest boat in the tred."

And at least the shortages of the Second War gave

us one of the few creations in Scottish humorous literature which can begin to hold its place with Para Handy and his world: the whisky starved island community with its wily Gaels and its blundering bureaucrats which are the magic ingredients in Compton Mackenzie's *Whisky Galore*.

The Para Handy
Stories

—

CHAPTER 8

The Vital Spark

Neil Munro tells us nothing about the age or origins of Para Handy's command. We know the skipper has spent some years with her as he is now serving under the puffer's second – unnamed – owner. It is perhaps reasonable to assume that his "fleet" runs to more than just the one vessel, as we learn (in *I/11 – Para Handy's Apprentice)* that the owner has a city centre office, in which the payment of wages is handled by a cashier – which would argue ownership of a number of ships.

We do know that the **Vital Spark** belonged to the sea-going class of puffer. Her crew of four, and the frequent references to her trips to Islay, Mull and Barra vouch for that. She would most likely have been one of the classic 66 ft. boats and probably have been built at Hay's Kirkintilloch yard. The firm built for many independent owners as well as for their own fleet.

As for her actual name, we know that the "Vital Spark" is of course the breath of life itself and that the phrase was first coined by the English poet Alexander Pope in his poem *The Dying Christian to his Soul,* which was precisely the sort of lugubrious but mournfully uplifting source that a contemplative Victorian moralist/capitalist might well trawl in search of an appropriate name for his latest investment.

> "Vital spark of Heav'nly flame!
> Quit, oh quit this mortal frame:

Trembling, hoping, ling'ring, flying,
Oh the pain, the bliss of dying!"

* * * * *

There was little danger of Para's **Vital Spark** flying. Her bluff bowed 66 ft. hull would have had a beam of almost 18 ft. and when fully laden she would have drawn, at maximum, about 9 ft. She would have been steered from a tiny open bridge, with canvas breakers, constructed aft of the funnel on top of the engine-room. She would have had one single, substantial mast with a steam-driven derrick, and she would have carried canvas for added sail power though she would have rarely deployed it.

In simplest terms she was indeed, as Para handy described her in the very first of the tales, "aal hold". Her cargo space came first, the engine-room second, the ill-provided-for crew a poor third. For'ard of the hold lay their accommodation. In a triangular space with roughly equilateral sides of about 18 ft. were crammed four wooden bunks, plus a table, benches, cupboards for stores and dunnage, and a coal-burning stove which doubled for heating and cooking. This was for generations of puffermen the basic and little-changing living space which so horrified the newly-wed mate's wife when she came a-visiting to Innellan. *[I/5]*

But, of course, beauty is always in the eye of the beholder. To Para Handy, and this is one of his most endearing and enduring attributes, his work-battered puffer had the grace, space and pace of a steam yacht and he would defend her blindly even – or more accurately, perhaps, particularly – in the face of the most scathing critics.

At times the skipper's praises for the little vessel are lyrical: at others, depending on the circumstances, they are defensive. There were four main areas of contention and of criticism of the **Vital Spark** and her characteristics, and thus four for our consideration.

Horse-drawn buses meeting the steamer

Typical of the McCrory brothers' totally unposed photographs this pierhead scene really captures the expectant bustle of a busy steamer terminal : note the furled sails of the coaster in the background.

King Edward coming alongside the pier

Of particular interest for showing in close-up the bridge with the skipper judging his approach, this picture also proves how prosperous hatters must have been in Edwardian Scotland!

Three's company!

A steamer excursion was the most popular holiday activity on the Clyde at the turn of the century – but the lady on the left looks as if she might just be a little worried about the risk of rough waters ahead.

Harvesting was hard work for all

Life was demanding, whether ashore or afloat : getting the harvest in while the weather was fair called for the unstinting efforts of the whole farming community in the days before the mechanisation of agriculture.

Lifeboat ready for moving overland

A scene straight out of "The Phantom Horse and Cart" [III/6] – "When was the good-man sober last?" "The year they took the lifeboat over the Machrihanish : he was at the cairtin' o't."

Steamer loading at West Loch Tarbert

The little Handa taking freight and passengers on board for Islay. Launched in 1878, she was known as "MacBrayne's Gladstone Bag" on account of her remarkable cargo carrying capacity : her beam was almost a quarter of her overall length!

Argyllshire Wedding Party

"I'll wudger there wasna another weddin' like it in Kintyre for generations : The herrin' trawlers is not back at their work yet, and herrin's up ten shullin's a box in Gleska." ("Para Handy's Wedding" [I/25])

All aboard!

This remarkable photograph of a holiday crowd thronging aboard an unidentified steamer repays close examination. There is always something new to be found in it and its portrayal of the life of the turn-of-the-century Clyde is so overwhelming as to be almost tangible.

Carters queue to unload barley

This was Campbeltown harbour in the days when the town boasted more than twenty distilleries. Barley shipments were almost a daily occurence and much came by puffer from the east coast farmlands. This consignment has come from further afield on a sea-going tramp steamer.

A great day out

A Clyde character who could almost be a stand-in for Para Handy is clearly enjoying himself on board an unknown steamer, though it is doubtful if he was a holidaymaker. He may be travelling to visit friends or family, or to a new job.

A rather grand band

The characteristic "German Bands" which entertained passengers in the steamers' hey-day certainly did not normally run to a harp and a double bass : this was probably a specially hired group for a charter outing.

Carradale Pier on Fair Day

It is the annual fete at the village of Carradale on the Mull of Kintyre and a steamer edges into the pier, probably packed with visitors from Campbeltwon at the south end of the peninsula.

Transferring cargo to a flit-boat

Many of the smaller lochside communities had no pier and though puffers carrying bulk cargos could beach to load or unload, the steamers transferred mail, packages and passengers to shore on boats rowed out from the local landing-stage.

Main Street, Campbeltown
Britain's most isolated town was a confident, self-sufficient community with a bustling and prosperous economy. It was almost totally dependent on sea-borne communications.

King Edward overhauling Kintyre
In this strikingly atmospheric photograph the brand new turbine speedster is in Kilbrannan Sound, just about to overtake the graceful but slower Kintyre which had been in service for 35 years at the time this picture was taken in 1903.

First, her appearance.
Second, her speed.
Thirdly, her seagoing qualities.
Fourthly, her status in the shipping hierarchy.

* * * * *

As to the first, it is established early on in the stories that the skipper is quite totally obsessed with keeping the puffer looking at her best. In our day the nearest equivalent to such overweening love for an inanimate object (though I would tend to agree with those who believe that ships, in truth, do have a soul) are the car-owners whose idea of Saturday morning fun is to busy themselves with bucket and chamois leather and, additionally, to treat the object of their admiration and affection to the occasional accessory.

Para Handy is therefore forever cajoling the crew to get out the paint tins or the tar pot whenever circumstances give them some idle time, but usually with little success. Indeed he has none at all when he tried to rouse them to spring-clean her at Ormidale pier *[II/7]*. "There it is again," says Macphail, who in fact never took any hand in the painting operations that did go on, "A chap canna get sittin' doon five meenutes in this boat for a read to himsel' withoot somebody breakin' their legs to find him a job". Even the usually loyal Dougie is on the side of the Philistines on this occasion: "Ye think it's great sport to be tar-tar-tarring away at the ship. Ye never consult either oor healths or oor inclinations."

In fact the skipper has two objectives: the first is to keep his boat looking cared for, the second to have her looking smart. This latter he is quite happy to do at his own expense. We have to ask ourselves if the owner knew how fortunate he was in having such a paragon for a skipper!

To achieve the first of these, pungent black tar would be the only raw material required, and this would be provided by the owner – and in copious quantity. "My goodness!" says Para as they complete several days of repainting the hull, "ye wouldna' think she would take such a desperate lot o' tar!"

But just as a baker will take pride in the way in which he is able to present a cake made from even the humblest of ingredients, so Para spared neither effort, nor inroads on his personal finances, to set the **Vital Spark** before the world in the manner befitting to his dreams of her status. Thus in order to fulfil his second ambition – that she look smart – her coal black hull was highlighted by the application of yellow or gilt to the buffer strake which encircled her just below her bulwarks, while at the level of her water line she was given a broad band of scarlet.

At Ormidale, on the occasion referred to above, "her newly painted understrakes reflected in the loch like a mirror, making a crimson blotch in a scene that was otherwise winter-brown."

In *Freights of Fancy [III/17],* discussed below, we are told that "with his own good hand, and at his own expense, her proud commander had freshened up her yellow bead and given her funnel a coat of red as gorgeous as a Gourock sunset". Westward facing Gourock was renowned for its views of the dramatic disappearances of the sun behind the Cowal hills on the opposite shore of the estuary.

Gazing with pride on his handiwork on that occasion, Para Handy enthused: "If ye shut wan eye......ye would think she wass the **Grenadier**."

* * * * *

Her speed, on the other hand, was a matter of fact rather than a matter of opinion: though this did not deter the captain from again attributing qualities to the little ship which were quite beyond her capacity.

"She drawed four feet forrit and nine aft, and she could go like the duvvle..." is the very first description of her we are given. *[I/1].*

"I heard it put at five knots," suggests narrator Neil Munro maliciously.

"Five knots! Show me the man that says five knots, and I will make him swallow the hatchet. Six knots, ass sure ass my name iss MacFarlane."

But – until the day the owner has her boiler fixed – Para gets little support from the crew for any fantasies regarding her rate of knots. Sunny Jim reckons that "wi' a' the speed this boat can dae, she could'na run up a pend close if it started rainin'." Even the engineer complains to the skipper that "she couldna dash doon a waterfa'!"

They are not impressed by the skipper's assessment that the puffer is capable *[I/5]* of "six knots in a gale of wund if Macphail is in good trum, and maybe seven if it's Setturday and him in a hurry to get home."

However, even the complaining Macphail changes his tune *[II/8]* when the owner has a new boiler installed.

"Built like a lever watch!" he enthuses as he inspects the new installations. "We'll can get the speed oot of her noo. There's boats gaun up and doon the Clyde wi' red funnels, saloon cabins and German bands in them, that have'na finer engines........wi' us its speed."

Not really, sad to say. All her days the little boat would have had all the attributes of the real puffers: two speeds – dead slow and stop – especially with a full load, or when she was thumping into a head wind with a deck cargo or, sometimes even less controllably, running light with her bluff bows soaring out of the water to act like a sail – in reverse. All her days, sadly, nothing would change: and Para would have to continue to retreat below to hide his feelings whenever the **King Edward** or one of the other greyhounds of the firth swept past the struggling puffer as if she were lying at anchor.....

* * * * *

It's already been indicated that the puffers had pretty poor seagoing qualities. The **Vital Spark** could not be expected to be an exception though, of course, Para Handy was as ever unwilling to accept the blunt facts.

It is suggested to him that she is "ill to trim".

Trimming was a crucial factor in the way a ship, whatever her size or her cargo, was prepared for sea. Good trim depended on how the cargo was balanced, stowed, separated, prevented from moving or creeping. Badly trimmed she could be slowed down, her seagoing qualities affected or, in the worst case scenario, put into actual danger in rough weather. The responsibility, in most ships, for ensuring that cargo vessels were properly laden lay with the mate.

Load a "mixed" cargo incompetently, without taking into account the variables of weight and volume, and the vessel could end up down by the head, down by the stern or – least to be desired of all – with a list to port or starboard which could only get worse.

Load a bulk cargo, one able to shift in heavy weather like sand or gravel for example, without inserting the framing and boards which were designed to divide the hold into smaller compartments, and the cargo could "move" and create problems identical to those outlined above. Down by the head or down by the stern, or listing – and with even less chance of putting things right.

Para Handy protests vigorously at the slander on the puffer's characteristics. "You could trum her with the wan hand behind your back, and you lookin' the other way."

Puffers were also notorious for being "wet" boats. Given a laden freeboard of mere inches, and a hull form which punched and fought its way through the water rather than sliding across it, this would have been inevitable.

Except, of course, in the case of the **Vital Spark**.....

"Wet! She would not take in wan cup of water unless it wass for synin' oot the dishes," insists her skipper. "She wass that dry she would not wet a postage stamp unless we slung it over the side in a pail."

Needless to say, the truth aboard Para Handy's pride and joy and, indeed the truth aboard every puffer, was very different and though the stories of the **Vital Spark** are tales of kindly daylight and great humour, there are occasions when Neil Munro's immense gifts as a descriptive writer come bursting through, and when we get an inkling of just what the darker side of life could be like on the puffers when unrelenting winter weather set in, or the sudden summer storms blew wild.

Just read the first sentences of *A Lost Man [I/9]*:

"It was a dirty evening, coming on to dusk, and the **Vital Spark** went walloping drunkenly down Loch Fyne with a cargo of oak bark, badly trimmed. They staggered to every shock of the sea: the waves came over her quarter........they had struggled round the point of Pennymore, every moment looking bleaker......"

Or this excerpt from *Salvage for the Vital Spark [III/9]*:

"The vessel was rounding Ardlamont in a sou'-wester that set her all awash like an empty herring box. Over her snub nose combed appalling sprays: green seas swept her fore and aft: she was glucking with internal waters and her squat red funnel whooped dolorously with wind."

Anyone who has ever been afloat in foul weather, whether in a rowing boat or an Atlantic liner, will immediately relate with the atmosphere conjured up by those two extracts of Munro's writing only too well. He was too accomplished a wordsmith not to occasionally introduce a brief moment of frightening reality into what were, otherwise, tales of good and gentle humour, and the brighter side of life.

The puffer's seagoing qualities (or the lack of them) were well understood – if not by her besotted skipper!

* * * * *

And so to Para Handy's final area of self-deception and of fond imaginings: the question of the little vessel's status in the maritime hierarchy. There are two aspects for consideration in this area: first, what other people – those who encountered her in her daily trafficking – thought about the puffer: and secondly what Para flattered himself into believing about her.

How the world saw his command mattered quite desperately to him. He suffered the ups and downs of gratifying recognition or the humiliation of a shattered self-respect, from the highs induced by the stranded Flood family's first question *([I/8], Lodgers on a Houseboat)* – "When does this steamer start?" to the lows of Dougie's wife's opening remarks on her first sight of the puffer *([I/5], The Mate's Wife)* – "I don't think muckle o' yer boat. I thocht it was a great big boat, wi' a cabin in it. Instead o' that, it's jist a wee coal yin."

To his detractors Para would go to any lengths to persuade them of the error of their ways. To Dougie's wife, for instance: "She's the most namely ship in the tred......men often come to take photographs of her. She has the lines of any steamboat of her size coming out of the Clyde. If her lum wass painted yellow and she had a bottom strake or two of green, you would take her for a yat." On being found by Neil Munro laden with a very mixed cargo indeed bound for Campbeltown: "To be puttin' scrap-iron and flittin's in a fine smert boat like this iss carryin' coals about in a coach." When Sunny Jim is, unusually for someone of his pleasant disposition, gratuitously off-hand about the puffer: "She might be a common gabbart for aal the pride Jum has in her."

Pride in his command was important to Para, but loyalty to her was the most important virtue of all. Such was his blind love for the **Vital Spark**. This was seen in practical terms by the willingness with which he spent his own money to ensure she looked her best, and in more intangible ways when his daydreams about her could overtake the reality.

Inevitably, that was a weakness of which the crew were more than once tempted to take advantage, but never to greater effect than in the story *Freights of Fancy [III/17]* when an entire tale is given over to his seduction into dreaming of turning the puffer into a cruise ship. For passengers.

The whole episode is sparked off by Para's remark, following a repainting and sprucing up of the boat, that "...if ye shut wan eye and glance end-on, ye would think she wass the **Grenadier**."

By the end of the story, Dougie, Sunny Jim and (surprisingly in that he but rarely takes part in the gentle teasing which is typical of the puffer crew's daily round) Dan Macphail himself have persuaded Para that the **Vital Spark** would be an ideal stand-in for the paddlers which are away on naval service – the story is set during the First War.

Para is measuring the deck space with a length of string to plan how best to accommodate his new cargo, discussing musical entertainment and the provision of teas, planning to store passengers' luggage in the hold, and dismissing the notion of moonlight cruises because "they slip past ye in the dark withoot a ticket"

Eventually, Dougie suffers from remorse at having wakened so many unattainable dreams, and the captain is bumped back down to earth.

But it is a pleasant memory of the **Vital Spark**, and a perfect example of the sheer joy and pride in command that characterise her skipper, if we join him for a moment in thinking *[III/17]* what might – just might – have been.

"His eye swept over her bulging hull, with the tar still wet and glistening on it: the bright new yellow stripe which made her so coquettish: the crimson funnel......[He] imaginatively peopled the narrow deck with summer trippers.....and glowed all over at the thought of his beloved vessel taking the quay at Dunoon on a Saturday afternoon with a crowd of the genteelest passengers.......

"The Captain's visage fell. His dream dispelled.

"But man, I aalways had the notion that the **Vital Spark** wass meant for something better than for cairryin' coals."

CHAPTER 9

Who was Para Handy?

P ara Handy is one of the greatest characters ever created in humorous fiction. If that seems an over statement, remember this: the stories of his exploits first appeared in print almost ninety years ago and, to the best of my knowledge, have remained in print in one form or another ever since.

There were other, vaguely comparable nautical or semi-nautical characters appearing in fictional escapades at round about the same time. The London Docks Night Watchman and the Coasting Bargees created in England by W. W. Jacobs come immediately to mind. They featured in a whole series of humorous stories of similar length to those of Neil Munro – usually with a strong maritime theme – and in them, just like Para Handy, they were frequently the narrators.

But, highly popular though they were at the time and indeed for some decades afterwards, where are they now? Para Handy and the **Vital Spark**, on the other hand, have stood the acid test of time as few other creations in fictional literature have done.

Though the chapters which follow try to suggest lightheartedly something of the nature and characteristics of the puffer's regular crew, and of the enigmatic Hurricane Jack, I don't think there is much point in trying to categorise Para Handy and all his attributes in a similar way. For one thing, it would be a long, long chapter if one did: he appears in all but one of the 99 tales and, in almost every one of them, we are learning something new about the man. The best way to get to know the skipper, and the intriguing complexity of his character, is to read the stories.

In this chapter, I would like instead to offer a thought on the identity of the man. In other words, to ask whether he had a prototype in real life, someone whom Neil Munro knew and on whom he based his most famous creation? There has been much discussion of this question over the years though, so far as I know, the theory which is advanced here has never been published before save in a letter to the *Glasgow Herald* some years ago: a letter written by the late father of the man who has provided me with the facts on which the theory is based. My hope is that this won't be thought of as too serious a way in which to enjoy the character of the fictitious skipper. If he really is founded on a known individual, that surely makes him of even more interest and value.

* * * * *

First of all though, we should at least summarise the character of Para Handy the puffer skipper. He is, like most of mankind, a man of contrasts and contradictions and that very human failing is one of his most attractive and believable traits. He is at once generous – but tight fisted: kind-hearted – but capable of sharp-tongued hurtfulness: frank and open in most of his dealings, he can be sly and furtive when it suits him: though he sees himself as a confident leader, he is vulnerable to many doubts and imagined fears: fond of a dram and a spree, he can in retrospect be very self-critical of his misdemeanours: bold when the mood is on him, he will at other times be timid to a fault: usually easy-going, he can sometimes lose his temper in a flash for no good reason whatsoever.

Thus the man who happily abandons any thoughts of a claim for substantial salvage money for retrieving the gabbart **Katharine-Anne** in *Salvage for the Vital Spark [II/6]* will try to sneak his way into *The Leap Year Ball [III/13]* because he grudges paying his half-crown.

He can veer from the unstinted affection he showers on *Wee Teeny [I/4]* to the torrent of verbal abuse which he is capable of directing against Dan Macphail at almost any time, at the drop of a hat. The man who tolerates to a fault the inertia of the crew supposedly under his command *(A Night Alarm [I/16])* can in a matter of seconds hurl the unwittingly offensive, fast-talking cockatoo to its doom in *An Ocean Tragedy. [II/10]*

* * * * *

Just precisely because Para Handy's character is so believable and so very human, it is inevitable that there are thoughts that here, surely, is a fictional creation which must have been based on a real person, on someone known to Neil Munro.

There has been speculation about this possibility for many years but the only positive "identification", or more accurately, "guesstimate" in published form of which I am aware is the theory advanced half-a-century ago in a booklet published by the *Campbeltown Courier*. What makes this particularly fascinating is that here are theories about Para Handy's alter ego which were being aired just a decade or so after the death of his creator. The search for the role model is far from being a recent phenomenon.

The booklet in question is *Campbeltown Yesterday* by A. Wylie Blue, and it was published in 1942. The author is writing about Campbeltown and its people and way-of-life at the turn of the century, and the relevant extract is as follows:

"Probably the most popular boat our Campbeltown generation of 50 years ago knew was the **Kintyre**.......with lines as graceful as those of a greyhound. The crew were mostly veterans....There was the skipper's room where Captain Peter MacFarlane's stout and hefty frame left little spare space in its limited bounds.

"Peter loved a crack....robust hilarity shook him when a good story was told.....

"He was a great natural. Some said that he served as

the original of Neil Munro's Para Handy. It was also whispered that Para Handy was not to be mentioned in Peter's presence. Whether Neil Munro had him in his eye when he immortalised the skipper of the **Vital Spark** in Para Handy, he has preserved a type of which our Peter was a notable and worthy representative. His burly form, his round, full, ruddy and red-whiskered countenance, his roar of command and his oracular pronouncements made memorable the arrival of the **Kintyre** at the piers of her route....

"To holidaymakers....he was an unfailing delight. He greeted them jovially from the bridge, assured them that 'Jamaica Bridge has'na come doon yet' or that 'The Queen [Victoria] has ordered the Provost not to be wearin' the kilt when he caals at Holyrood. "He hasna the legs" says the Queen.'"

Now, the suggestion that this particular steamer captain, who retired in 1916 as skipper of the **Davaar**, was the original Para Handy has got one or two things going for it: but I submit that it's got a whole lot more going against it.

On the plus side, the real and the imagined captains seem to have shared a sense of humour and a fondness for their fellow men: so do most people, however. They were also of vaguely similar appearance if we can judge by the one very brief description of Para Handy which Neil Munro gives – "a short, thick-set man with a red beard." While the real captain of the **Kintyre** is certainly similarly "red-whiskered", however, his size is categorised as being "stout and hefty" and I think that be-tokens something rather more substantial than the "short, thick-set" frame ascribed to Para Handy.

On the minus side I suggest that the evidence that this is not the man on whom Para Handy was based is quite overwhelming.

First, there is the matter of geography. The **Kintyre** was a Campbeltown steamer and her skipper, though originally from Tarbert (to which community he would return on his retirement in 1916), was based there. The **Kintyre** maintained the Campbeltown to Glasgow service as a combined passenger and cargo vessel in consort with the first **Dalriada** and the **Kinloch.** Each journey was a full day's steaming, with many intermediate ports of call.

Communications between Campbeltown and Inveraray were non-existent by sea, and tortuous and sporadic by road, during the author's formative teenage years around 1880 before he moved to Glasgow. There was no way by which Neil Munro could have come to hear about, never mind to know at first hand, the foibles or pleasantries of a steamer skipper so remote from his own home.

Secondly I am sure that what might at first hearing seem the most telling argument in favour of Captain Macfarlane being the prototype for Para is, on a moment's reflection, rather the most convincing reason for dismissing the whole idea.

Neil Munro would never have wittingly given Para Handy, Peter MacFarlane, the very same name as the real man, whoever he was, upon whom he was modelled. Had Para in fact been built up round the character of the skipper of the Kintyre, he would most certainly have been given a different name!

It's not surprising, though, that Wylie Blue suggests that "It was whispered that Para Handy was not to be mentioned in Peter's presence." I would just bet it wasn't! The unfortunate skipper was probably the butt of a host of allusions and sly nudges and winks, and would be understandably furious about the (albeit coincidental) circumstance which had given a popular comic hero a name identical to his own and made him an object of curiosity to locals and visitors alike. Steamer captains were respected members of the community at the time and, if as genial as Captain MacFarlane seems to have been, they were popular characters as well. But they were certainly not figures of fun. Neil Munro the experienced working journalist would never have knowingly created a situation so charged with the potential for embarrassing one of their number and thus with due respect to the folk of Campbeltown, I do not think "their man" could possibly have been the real Para Handy.

That is particularly so when a much more likely candidate, and one who was regarded as the Para Handy prototype *even while the stories were being penned,* has been put forward by someone with access to the authenticity of a tradition which has been passed down through the generations: a direct descendant.

* * * * *

Eoin McArthur is now retired and living on the shores of upper Loch Fyne. His forbears, members of a large but close-knit family, have for generations past lived on the lochside and in the town of Inveraray itself. So, of course, did Neil Munro's own forbears. More: the Munros and the McArthurs were always very close. Eoin McArthur, indeed, is himself distantly related to the creator of Para Handy: his paternal grandfather Daniel married Isabella Munro of Inveraray who was a second cousin of Neil. Going even further back, we find that Neil Munro's grandfather was one of the same McArthur kin.

The two "clans" have been closely associated for several generations. Eoin still corresponds today with Neil Munro's surviving grand-daughter. She, too, confirms from the Munro dynasty the belief long held as fact within the McArthur family: that one of their number provided the model for the immortal puffer skipper – a man who would have been known to Neil Munro during his impressionable early years in Inveraray, during his latter schooldays, and in his first years of working experience in the lawyer's office in the town.

This man was an uncle of Eoin's grandfather Daniel McArthur. He had several brothers, but he is "our man" beyond reasonable doubt. His name was Peter McArthur and he lived at Drishaig on the western shore of Loch Fyne a few miles north of Inveraray. He seems never to have married and in successive censuses he is described as a "fisherman". His household also contained his mother and, after her death, one or more of his sisters. He had a boat, the **Dan Todd**, and it is thought that this may have been a general purpose skiff. He had some land at Drishaig and presumably would require to ferry stock or feed or produce to and from Inveraray, in addition to pursuing a living at the fishings.

Perhaps the most telling factor in leading to the conclusion that here was a prime candidate for Neil Munro's veritable role-model is that Peter's father was Alexander McArthur: and that "Para Handy", in the Highland patois of the period, was a diminutive for "Peter, son of Sandy (i.e. Alexander)"

Peter McArthur was born in 1817, which puts him in his late fifties and early sixties when Neil Munro could have known him and it is surely certain that he did. In *The Brave Days,* the collection of Munro's autobiographical essays collected and edited by George Blake in the year after his death, the first of them all contains the following passage:

"The snow will be deep in Glencaldine today: it is just such weather as we loved in March when we had to put on an extra waistcoat and carry a peat thro' the drifts to old John McArthur's school.....our dominie was a gentleman of culture."

Difficult to imagine that, in a remote Highland community one hundred and twenty years ago, this particular McArthur would not be related in some way to the others: easy to see that through John his teacher, Neil Munro might get to know Peter or at least get to know something about him. His reputation as a man with a fondness for a spree, relates Eoin McArthur, has been passed down the generations: among other exploits in pursuit of happiness, he would regularly sail across the loch from Drishaig – to get to the Inns at Cairndow. The whole McArthur family of that generation, says Eoin, were thought to be more light-hearted and fun-loving than their more douce contemporaries the Munros.

For all their cheerful disposition, however, the McArthur family of Eoin's childhood, he recalls, were none too happy at the identification of one of their immediate forbears as Munro's inspiration. Para's love of a dram and of a spree perhaps sat less happily with that particular McArthur generation which, after years of largely farming and fishing activity, was now producing professional men who were beginning to take themselves more seriously, and perhaps felt just a little bit embarrassed by the connection.

Sadly but really not surprisingly there is no hard, written evidence that would confirm this connection: but the oral tradition in the McArthur family goes back to the days when the stories were being set down and has been passed from generation to subsequent generation: and to this very day Neil Munro's own descendants endorse it as well.

One last piece of evidence, admittedly "negative" evidence, is contained actually within the stories and certainly helps to confirm my own feeling that the McArthur connection is probably the right one. Only once in the 99 tales is Inveraray identified as the setting for a story despite the fact that the town on the Fyne was the author's place of birth and up-bringing. It must have been at the centre of his universe in his formative years, and of his thoughts as he set down the escapades of the fun-loving skipper of the **Vital Spark**. It is as if he was deliberately excluding any reference to Inveraray for fear of pointing the reader towards the place where he had experienced actual events or known real characters on which he was now drawing to create his fictional world.

* * * * *

As a postscript to this speculative essay I find that it is very strange, almost bizarre indeed, that that single reference to Inveraray in the stories has an unnerving parallel to Neil Munro's own circumstances. He was born out of wedlock to Ann Munro, who was a kitchen maid at Inveraray Castle, seat of the Dukes of Argyll. The identity of his father remains unknown to this day.

In *In Search of a Wife [I/13]*, the one and only story set in Inveraray, Para Handy and Dougie are trying to find a bride for The Tar, who is too blate to do any courting for himself.

"'My Chove,' said Para Handy, 'I have the very article that would fit you.'

"'What's – what's her name,' asked The Tar, alarmed at the way destiny seemed to be rushing him into matrimony.

"'Man, I don't know,' said the Captain, 'but she's the laandry-maid up here in the Shurriff's – chust a regular beauty.'"

Am I alone in finding it somewhat extraordinary, not to say uncanny, that the son of an unmarried kitchen maid at Inveraray Castle should, in the only reference to the town of his birth in the whole Para Handy repertoire, build the story round the wooing of a laundry maid at the Sheriff's Hall – an Inveraray household probably second only in status and grandeur to the Castle itself – in what seems almost a bizarre allusion to his own mother's circumstances?

* * * * *

To end on an appropriately lighter note, remember and enjoy the very vivid description we have of Para in the opening paragraphs of the first story.

Though it was published in book form as *Para Handy, Master Mariner* it originally appeared in the *Glasgow Evening News* of January 16, 1905 titled *The Ancient Mariner:* not nearly such a friendly name – one can see why it was later changed."A short, thick-set man with a red beard, [and] a hard round felt hat, ridiculously out of harmony with a blue pilot jacket and trousers and a seaman's jersey........humming to himself a song that used to be very popular on gabbarts, but is now gone out of date.......by that sign, and by his red beard, and by a curious gesture he had, as if he were now and then going to scratch his ear and only determined not to do it when his hand was up, I knew he was one of the Macfarlanes."Surely a precise pen-portrait: surely from the life?

CHAPTER 10

The Crew

Neil Munro manned the **Vital Spark** with a nicely contrasting set of characters for a crew. There is little or no physical description of them, a definite plus point which allows every reader to decide on an appropriate and personal mental picture of each one – but their nature, their foibles, their good and bad points, are carefully set out. The interplay between such a diverse collection of men is one of the great strengths of the tales: the humour created by the story-lines is greatly enhanced by the added dimension of the very believable relationships and reactions of such a motley gang.

Dougie Campbell the mate is Para's staunchest ally and, with only rare exceptions, a kindly and good-natured figure, prepared to live and let live. He usually lets others (particularly Para Handy of course) do the leading, which he will follow: but on occasion, as in the opening story of the crew's prolonged spree in Greenock, he can be the instigator of both fun and trouble. He is not a very good sailor: timid, the skipper calls him more than once, and his fear of heavy weather makes it almost certain that he has never been seagoing, but always confined his maritime career to the relatively sheltered waters of the Firth and adjacent coasts and islands.

Dan Macphail, engineer in charge of the most unreliable set of machinery on the river, is more charismatic. He and Para Handy are as often as not at loggerheads and both can be totally unfeeling in the remarks they make about each other. Dan is sentimental – as his devotion to and emotional involvement with his penny novelettes demonstrates: but he also has a sharp tongue and, as something of a misanthrope, will often distance himself from the rest of the crew. He has been deep sea before joining the puffer and can be contemptuous about the set of engines which he now has to tend. By contrast again, he can be very defensive of them, and of his abilities as an engineer.

Dougie and Dan are with the **Vital Spark** throughout her career but – for reasons unknown – Neil Munro changes the fourth crew member, the deckhand, at the end of the first collection.

The first deckhand is Colin Turner, usually referred to by his unexplained by-name of The Tar. He is about half the age of the others and thus sometimes put upon by them. Generally portrayed (and with considerable justification) as extremely lazy and somewhat ham-fisted, he is a pleasant enough but rather inarticulate and introverted character.

Davie Green – always known as Sunny Jim – takes over as The Tar's replacement in the first story of the second collection and is in complete contrast to his predecessor. Jim is outgoing and extrovert, cheerful to the point of being mischievous, and no respecter of age, experience or traditions, as many of his exploits well demonstrate. There is no doubting how he came by his nickname, or its appropriateness.

Jack Maclachlan – Hurricane Jack – was never employed as an official member of the crew on the **Vital Spark**: many of the exploits which he and Para Handy shared and which are recounted by the skipper actually took place prior to his appointment to the captaincy of the puffer. However, Jack appears as an occasional stand-in or as an extra man and, in the "fiction-within-fiction" tales of the **Vital Spark** as Mystery Ship, he is portrayed as being in overall charge of the operations.

These were Para Handy's crew and the raw materials round which Neil Munro created some of the most entertaining and timeless humorous stories ever penned. The most intriguing of them all is Hurricane Jack and he merits a chapter to himself. Meanwhile it is well worth taking a more detailed look at his shipmates.

* * * * *

Dougie is Para's closest friend and staunchest ally among the crew but I feel we really learn less about him than we do about any of the others. At an early stage it is evident that on all but a few occasions his personality will, sadly, always be over-shadowed by that of Para Handy himself.

He has his moments, and splendid ones they are: a favourite mental picture is the one conjured up by Munro's account of the outrageously drunk Dougie breenging into the big schoolhouse at Castlebay to give the children "a lecture on music and the curse of drink, with illustrations on the trump." *A Desperate Character [I/17]*.

More often than not, though, Dougie is being put upon, usually by Para Handy, always with the uncritical support of the rest of the crew. Henpecked at home he obviously was and though he probably regarded his spells on the puffer as a relief from that and from the pressures of life in a Plantation tenement with ten kids, he was really exchanging one form of hen-pecking for another. Dougie deserves, and gets, our sympathy even when we feel that what he really needs is a good shaking.

He has sailed with Para Handy for many years: he was already the **Vital Spark**'s mate when he got married and, early on in the stories, we learn that he is father of ten children, *(Dougie's Family [I/20]* with another on the way. The other turns out to be "twuns".

So he has been Para's mate for at least eleven years, and it is pretty certain that as mate he will remain. Dougie just does not have the urge, or the edge, to progress to his own command. There is no suggestion that he has ever been anything other than a coastal waters sailor all his life. A man of extreme caution in much of his doings, he is fearful in bad weather, nervous in wartime, timid when authority confronts or bureaucracy threatens. Thus he is often a reluctant participant in some of the nefarious goings-on of the crew, unless of course he is on one of his sporadic but monumental off-the-Rechabite-wagon sprees, when he himself is probably the ring-leader. He is also sadly gullible and prone to be the butt of practical joking which the others would not have stood for. It's poor Dougie who has to wear a "skirt" in *The Land Girls [III/ 10]* and so lose a bet, and his new boots, to Hurricane Jack: it's Dougie who is wound up to near hysteria in *Commandeered [III/20]* when the others convince him that the puffer has been taken over by the admiralty as a canal block-boat, and they're to sail her to the Kiel Canal and scuttle her: it's Dougie who is set up by Para Handy as a sitting-duck for the hypnotist at the Tarbert fair. *(Queer Cargoes [I/62])*

The other side of the coin, of course, is that Dougie is by far the kindliest and most sympathetic of any of the crew and there is a gentleness and even an air of resignation about him. It is as if he knows that, with the occasional glorious exception, he will be the eternal straight-man to the wily peccadilloes of his crewmates and, above all, his skipper: the butt of their jokes and their favourite target for an unmalicious teasing.

Sadly, as is always the case with life, it is the imps and not the angels who interest us most. The rest of the crew are much more individual and varied characters, more three-dimensional, more fleshed out. Dougie's main role in the stories is as the ever-present anchor-man who gives some continuity to the unfolding of the plots – incidents to which he is more often the witness and corroborator rather than the instigator.

* * * * *

Macphail the misanthrope is a character of contrasts. He and Para Handy can be critical of each other's abilities and character to the point of personal abuse.

Sometimes Macphail is the loudest to condemn the puffer as a floating disaster zone but elsewhere he can leap to her defence.

On occasion he can be the ringleader of a particular ploy – such as the purchase and dispatch of the mock Valentine in *The Valentine that Missed Fire [I/23]:* at other times he seems to be cold-shouldered by the rest of the crew, as in *The Tar's Wedding [I/18]* where he has been left to guard the puffer while the rest go off to the reception party. The skipper and engineer appear to be at serious loggerheads at this point, for even at the wedding party Para Handy can't resist a verbal attack on the absent man with: "I have a ship yonder....that I left in charge of an enchineer by the name of Macphail, no' to be trusted with such a responsibulity".

It is certain that Macphail had been deep sea earlier in his career. There are references to voyages to Africa (the Congo), South America (the river Plate), Italy (where he saw macaroni hung up to dry in Genoa), the Baltic (where he saw Russians eating raw herring) and an un-named Levant port with a cargo of "Mahomedan pilgrims". There is even a suggestion that some of his deep water service might have been in the Navy. In *Para Handy has an Eye to Business [II/7]* he reacts to the skipper's efforts to persuade the crew to refurbish some paintwork by complaining "There it is again! A chap canna get sittin' doon five meenutes. Ye micht as well be in a man-o'-war."

The great mystery about Dan Macphail, of course, is the question of whether or not he had blood on his hands.....

The first reference to this possibility comes in *The Sea Cook [I/7]* when Para Handy mentions as an aside to The Tar that "the enchineer wance killed a man in the Australian bush." Then in *A Night Alarm [I/16]* we learn that Para Handy "...was afraid of the engineer because that functionary had once been on a ship that made a voyage to Australia, and used to say that he had killed a man in the Bush. When he was not sober it was two men, and he

would weep." However, Macphail himself contradicts all
this in *The Fortune Teller [II/12]* when the skipper and
mate are avoiding him like the plague after a fortune-teller
at the Tarbert Fair had told them both to "beware o' a man
wi' black whiskers that came from Australia." "Ye're a
couple of Hielan' cuddies," says the engineer: "Man, I
never wass nearer Australia than the River Plate." That
statement is the nearest we come to knowing the truth
about Macphail's secret past – if indeed he had one!

As the only member of the crew with literary pretensions the engineer is an avid reader – of the trashy
romantic novelettes popular at the period. Far from re-
specting his literacy the crew in general, and the captain
in particular, are highly offensive about it and Para Handy
can send Macphail off to sulk in solitude in his engine-
room by alluding to the engineer's sentimentality: he had
once given himself away and never been allowed to forget
it. Neil Munro has Para Handy close an argument *(The Sea
Cook [I/7])* with the following passage :

"'Hoo's Lady Fitzgerald's man getting on?' This
last allusion was to Macphail's passion for penny fiction,
and particularly to a novelette story over which the engineer had once been foolish enough some years before to
show great emotion."

There are hints that Macphail might have had vague
pretensions to being something of a dandy. This is quite
often the case where a man has a "dirty" job – there were
few dirtier than that of engineer on a coal-burning Clyde
puffer – and likes to contrast that by putting on something
of a show when off duty. He seems, for a start, to have been
the only man on board who possessed a mirror. In *The
Malingerer [I/3]* Dougie's response to the Tar's question
"Am I lookin' very bad?" is: "Bad's no' the name for it,
chust look at yourself in the enchineer's looking-gless."
That this was the only one on board is surely confirmed
when in *The Mate's Wife [I/5]* a mirror is one of the
purchases which Dougie's better half makes to brighten
up the gloomy fo'c'sle. On another occasion *(The Baker's*

Little Widow [I/21]) Para Handy, dressing up to go courting, on one of the rare occasions upon which he wore a
topcoat, "envied Macphail his Cairngorm scarfpin."

At once the most intriguing and the most damning
indication of the engineer's hankering for a more genteel
life comes in the classic story of *The Mudges [III/15]*
where Macphail – elsewhere established as a married man
with five of a family – is "walking out" with one Mima
Macrae whenever the puffer calls at Arrochar. Twenty
times he's been calling on her, says Para Handy, and she
still does not know that he is as bald as a coot, as the vain
suitor never takes his cap off. The suggestion of some
extra-marital activity is an astonishing one, given the
official moral code of the era in which Neil Munro was
writing, and the family readership who were the consum-
ers of the *Glasgow Evening News*. My own feeling is that
here is one of the very rare occasions when Munro slips up
on a matter of what the film-makers would refer to as
"continuity". Has it completely slipped his mind that
Macphail was married – a fact established early on in the
stories?

One other possible error of continuity follows when
Macphail gets his First War call-up papers. *(How Jim
Joined the Army [III/22]).* Surely Dan was far too old to
be on the conscription rosters? There are hints elsewhere
that he is in fact the oldest man on board, as when Para
pronounces *(Among the Yachts [II/16])* "Anything wi'
Macphail for sport....Ye would think at his time o' life,
and the morn Sunday, that his meditaations would be
different."

The engineer's is a difficult character to summarise.
Some of the unkindly remarks directed at him, and the
way in which he is sometimes excluded from the activities
and society of the rest of the crew, are the direct result of
his own misanthropic behaviour.

Most often, though, he comes across as a likeable
but rather lonely figure who deserves better treatment
from his mates and some kindly sympathy from the

reader. When the crew involve him in their conversation and their conviviality he is transformed from the morose figure sometimes to be found taking a jaundiced view of life from the depths of his engine-room. Even at his worst, though, he is never deserving of the bitter sarcasm of which Para Handy is capable, and the aspersions cast on his technical abilities – and his Lowland antecedents – are worse than unjust.

"Macphails!" the skipper exclaims to The Tar when informed that the lad is courting a girl from an Easdale family of that name *(In search of a Wife [I/13]):* "I never hear the name of Macphail but I need to scratch mysel'."

Poor Dan! Dougie the mate is the man who gets most of the reader's sympathy at the advantages taken of him: but he is in general a blind and uncomplaining follower of Para Handy in all the skipper says and does. Macphail's problems really stem from the fact that he has some independence of character and is prepared to show it. Whatever the cost to his pride and whatever hurt to his feelings!

* * * * *

The Tar is a much less complex character – one drawn merely in outline as it were, where Dan Macphail is a full portrait. Also The Tar, except for a brief reappearance from the private yacht which he has been crewing since leaving the **Vital Spark**, is only a member of the cast for the first 25 stories.

The mental picture conjured up is of a bulky young man, slow of movement and of little imagination. His first appearance *(The Malingerer [I/3])* sets the standard: he is trying to avoid the forthcoming task of loading a timber cargo in upper Loch Fyne by feigning illness. He duped the skipper – at least to begin with – but the mate never had any doubts about the idle nature of a man who "was usually as tired when he rose in the morning as when he went to bed." While it is The Tar who saves the day when

Wee Teeny [I/4] chokes on a sweet by thumping her on the back, this is only because the others are too fond of the wee girl to lay a finger on her but send for the Tar instead as "he hasna' mich feelin's."

Cooking is one of his main duties – and in this department too he shows himself devoid of imagination and with little or no enthusiasm for seeing that his crewmates are even tolerably catered for. It's no surprise that the Flood family *(Lodgers on a Houseboat [I/8])* also give his culinary efforts a very definite thumbs down, though he is a little more successful – and active – in pampering the owner's schoolboy son *(Para Handy's Apprentice [I/11])*

It would be interesting to know just what was the cause of the quarrel with Para Handy at the Furnace Ball that caused the skipper not just to sack him, but to give him a black eye as well! *[I/9]*. Indeed one wonders, given his almost total inarticulateness with the opposite sex – he has to enlist Para Handy and the mate to do his courting for him – just what he was doing at a Ball in the first place!

It is, however, laziness that marks him out. When the Flood's baby finally stops crying and goes to sleep "the only sound to be heard was the snore of The Tar." When he ventures the opinion *(Queer Cargoes [I/12])* that the strangest one he ever came across was a consignment of sawdust, the skipper remarks that "Sawdust would suit you fine....I'll warrant you got plenty of sleep that trup." When The Tar refuses to budge when the puffer's steam whistle goes off in the middle of the night Para sets about him with "Tar by by-name and Tar by nature! You will stick to your bed that hard they could not take you off without half-a-pound of salt butter." Even at his own wedding reception he went a-missing and was finally found "sound asleep on the top of a chest in the neighbour's house." *(The Tar's Wedding [I/18])* As the crew sup the ale paid for with the money Dougie raised by selling a coal-fish to a Glasgow Fair holidaymaker *(A Stroke of Luck [I/19])* "the mate contributed a reel and strathspey on the trump to the evening's programme, during which The Tar fell asleep."

His parting from the **Vital Spark** after the first series seems to have been amicable enough, though we are not given any details. He re-appears just once *(The Return of the Tar [II/11])* when he pays the puffer a visit in Campbeltown – and the final word on the attributes of The Tar is left to Para Handy, who suggests: "Come doon and I'll show you the same old bunk you did a lot o' sleepin' in."

* * * * *

Sunny Jim – Davie Green – was of a very different mould. He appears as the puffer's deckhand in all of the second series of stories, and as an occasional supercargo in the third (and some of the new Birlinn additions too) having apparently taken some sort of shore job – though what that might be we never learn. He then enlisted in the army during the First War. He was cheerful, lively, companionable and something of a prankster as well. The Birlinn editors have happily solved one mystery – why Sunny Jim rather than Sunny Davie? The adjective certainly suits his character so no quarrels there, but why change the name? The answer turns out to be that "Sunny Jim" in the contemporary real world was a well-known character from a long-running national advertising campaign for a brand of oatmeal: the equivalent of the Milky Bar Kid of Edwardian Scotland, perhaps: and thus the soubriquet became attached to Davie Green because he had a genuinely sunny character.

Previously with the Cluthas on the Upper Clyde, Sunny Jim had no pretensions to be a "proper" sailor and the misanthropic Macphail did not take kindly to him. "He's no' a sailor at a'! He's a clown: I've see'd better men jumpin' through girrs at a penny show". But the others loved him as a "most valuable acquisition", a man of "humour and resource" whose "finest gift was imagination." Para Handy said of him "It's a peety listenin' to such damned lies iss a sin, for there iss no doubt it is a most pleasant amusement!"

It was the resourceful Sunny Jim who cashed in on the earning potential of the stranded whale in *Treasure Trove" [II/4]:* the puckish Jim who performed the trick of the vanishing sausages in *A New Cook [II/1]:* the mischievous Jim who sent Para Handy home with a basketful of chuckie stones from a Tobermory beach to make "vegetarian" stock for the captain's wife in *A Vegetarian Experiment [II/8]:* the glib-tongued Jim who had Para Handy believing that his crime, when he slung the offending cockatoo over the side of the boat in *An Ocean Tragedy [II/10],* was manslaughter at best, murder at worst – because the bird could talk: the eye-on-the-main-chance Jim who set up the unsuccessful Petroloid testimonial scam in *The Hair Lotion [II/13],* and later the equally fruitless fake swimming marathon in Kilbrannan Sound in *To Campbeltown by Sea [II/21]:* the vindictive Jim who put the clocks forward three hours instead of one in *Summer-Time on the Vital Spark [III/18]* and deprived the skipper and mate of their Sunday morning lie-in: the devious Jim who took Macphail's place in the Scottish Fusiliers after he himself had been rejected because of his glass eye in *How Jim Joined the Army [III/22].*

In short, Jim engendered a great deal of entertainment and variety in the life of the puffer's crew. "Though they were sometimes the victims of his practical jokes," says Neil Munro in *Treasure Trove [II/4],* "the others of the crew forgave him readily because of the fun he made. It is true that when they were getting the greatest entertainment from him they were, without thinking it, generally doing his work for him....but at least he was better value for his wages than The Tar, who could neither take his fair share of the work nor tell a baur."

* * * * *

It is pleasant to be able to conclude this chapter with the thought that with the one exception of the night at

Furnace when the captain took a swipe at The Tar, this motley crew lived their years aboard the **Vital Spark** without any physical conflict and indeed in relative harmony, given the diversity of their characters and the strain of being cooped up in so small and so ill-equipped a living space. They were above all united as a team when it came to defending the reputation and the qualities of their floating home!

CHAPTER 11

Hurricane Jack

Of all the characters ever created by Neil Munro for his humorous fiction – whether for the Para Handy Tales, or those built round waiter/beadle Erchie Macpherson, or travelling salesman Jimmy Swan, Hurricane Jack must be the most intriguing and the most enigmatic.

He comes galumphing through Para Handy's world like some bacchanalian merry-andrew, a jovial poltergeist dispensing fun and happiness wherever he goes. If we are lucky, we can perhaps count one or two "Hurricane Jacks" in the coterie of our own friendships, the sort of charismatic people who carry a party around with them as part of their life's baggage, whose arrival anywhere, and at any time, is guaranteed to lift the spirits, cheer the heart and promise good times and a spree to come.

In my own life I count myself favoured indeed to have had the friendship of three people endowed with that elusive and quite priceless talent.

What particularly fascinates about Hurricane Jack is that such a well-rounded and very specifically chronicled character must surely be based on somebody of Neil Munro's acquaintance. Even more perhaps than Para Handy himself Jack is a very real and a very believable personality. Indeed, his spectacularly chequered career would be less credible as fiction than it would be as fact and could surely not simply have been invented! It is a very good example of reality surpassing imagination.

He is one of the few of Munro's characters whose

physical description is given – albeit very briefly. Although he takes part in a number of the stories which Para recounts in the first two collections it is a long time before Munro actually has us meeting him in person for the first time, in the opening episode in *Hurricane Jack of the Vital Spark*. Prior to that we have established something of his character and how he is held in almost reverent esteem and affection by the skipper. We have been given some inkling of his character but the only hint at his appearance has been in reference to his size. "Six feet three, and a back like a shippin'-box", as Para enthuses in *Piracy in the Kyles [II/15]*. By the end of the story Jack's dimensions have increased with the telling to such a degree that Macphail remarks "I'm gled I wasna' his tailor" with some justification! "He was six feet six," concludes the skipper, "and had a back on him like a Broomielaw shed."

The real Jack – "'John Maclachlan' in the books but 'Hurricane Jack' in every port from here to Callao" – *[III/1]* is described by Munro as "A lanky, weatherbeaten person with a tightly-buttoned blue serge suit and a very low-crowned bowler hat at an angle of forty-five" with "a hybrid accent, half-Scotch and half-American" and a bone-crushing handshake. While that is merely a short thumbnail sketch, it presents an immediate mental picture of the man and indeed an indication of the character of the man, and must surely have been taken from the life. At the time of this encounter Jack was either still going deep-sea, or had just stopped: he states that this is the first time he's been home "in three years." In a later story *(Land Girls [III/10])* we are told his age – 55. We already know that he is from Lochaline, a remote community on the Morvern shore of the Sound of Mull.

He and Para Handy are friends and shipmates of many years standing, and by sifting through the snippets of information given at various times in the 99 stories, it is possible to make a reasonable guess at the path of his career. It can only be described, charitably, as chequered: the uncharitable would term it a disastrous failure. The reasons for the ups-and-downs of Jack's life are to be explained by the type of man he was, and his character will be considered shortly. In the meantime, his biography goes something like this.

It's likely that the very first boat he and Para crewed together was the sailing gabbart **Margaret Ann** "that made money for a man in Tarbert" *[III/6]*. Next, they were about three or four years on the **Aggie**, and though it's never stated what type of boat this was, instinct suggests that this was also a sailing gabbart and that, from her, Jack moved on to become a skipper (for which no "lines" would have been required) on the sailing coaster **Janet** "before he started goin' foreign" *(The End of the World [III/28])*. It was probably from this command that Jack graduated to the clippers, initially as a deckhand on the passenger packets of the Black Ball Line. *[III/1]*. He must have studied for and passed the various examinations for his Mate's and then Master's Certificates, for he eventually became a clipper captain – on the **Dora Young** (a purely fictional craft so far as can be found out) and the **Port Jackson** – a real-life record-breaker built in Aberdeen in 1882. That Neil Munro places the fictional Jack on a factual windjammer does raise one intriguing speculation which may well be based on totally erroneous conjecture but which must at least be worth having a closer look at.

If there is any truth in my belief that the fictional character of Hurricane Jack was based on a real seaman of Neil Munro's acquaintance, might that person have sailed on the **Port Jackson** at some stage in his career? As a deckhand only though, not as an officer: had he had that status it would have identified my putative role model only too explicitly to his shipmates and contemporaries. But might not the author have "flagged" the real-life identity of the "man who was Hurricane Jack" to the man himself by introducing a reference to an actual voyage (the 39-day record-breaker is a matter of historical fact) in a well-known ship. Why else, one could ask, would such reality be suddenly injected into a series of tales which are otherwise the product of their author's fertile imagination?

Certainly the seagoing career of Hurricane Jack, whoever he may have been – if he existed at all – was varied to say the very least! Culling indications from various stories in the collection we can establish that he sailed to and from Australia in the wool trade: brought home tea from the China station ("he made the fastest passages in his time that wass ever made in the tea trade"): and sailed the Horn to the Pacific coast of South America for nitrates. He was also in India at some point and there is a suggestion that he commanded a smuggler "in America" *(Running the Blockade [BP/88])*. Since he was not old enough for this to have been the Civil War, this particular activity was probably undertaken during the Spanish-American war of 1898.

His ocean voyaging was punctuated by spells of work closer to home. At one time he was "home from the sea, and workin' a net wi' cousins that had a skiff [fishing boat] caaled the **Welcome Back**". *(Hurricane Jack's Luck-bird [III/7])*: he also crewed with Para Handy, in the days before the skipper had his post with the **Vital Spark**, on two other puffers. One, the **Julia**, seems to have been the boat Para was on immediately before getting his own command. *(Fog [II/17])*. The other, which is not identified as a puffer but must have been, since Para remarks that they "were not costing the owners much for coals if coals wass our cargo", was the **Elizabeth Ann,** "a boat that belonged to Girvan". *(Hurricane Jack [I/10])*. And there were other periods spent in the coasting trade about which we are told nothing, for Para Handy relates *(The End of the World [III/28])* that Jack "wass a born rover that asked for nothing better than to dodge aboot the Western Hielan's in his own dacent boat, or go percolatin' roond the Broomielaw wi' a cheery frien' or two when his vessel was in the Clyde."

An up and down career it indeed was, and sadly

almost the last we hear of Hurricane Jack (in *Sunny Jim Returns [BP/97])* is that he had spent the entire War "shovellin' coal in a depot ship": surely an ignominious and frustrating fate for one of the brightest stars in the whole galaxy of humorous fiction, though one portended earlier when Para first introduces Jack into the scenario by stating *(Hurricane Jack [I/10])* that "He wass captain of the **Dora Young,** wan of them cluppers: he's a hand on a gaabert the now, but aalways the perfect gentleman."

* * * * *

So what went wrong to turn such a promising career into an often depressing present and a very uncertain future?

Neil Munro gives us the answers to that question quite clearly and unmistakably. A weakness for a dram: a temper on a short fuse: and a cavalier and careless attitude towards such mundane matters as money. Those attributes have been the downfall of many who promised much, and indeed they could be regarded as the other side of the coin which marks the bearers of good cheer and a permanent party atmosphere like Hurricane Jack. Of the three folk of that happy disposition whom I have been lucky enough to know all were marked by exactly those same three character traits.

It is also very typical – as Para Handy well demonstrates – that the friends of characters like Hurricane Jack will almost always allow themselves to be blinded to their faults. Para's affection for his shipmate amounts almost to deification, and he will not willingly say or hear a word against him, though he will – albeit reluctantly – admit his friend's shortcomings to himself. When Jack makes his first appearance in the stories he speaks of him "in terms of admiration and devotion which would suggest that Jack is a sort of demi-god" *[I/10]* though in the course of the stories the truth comes out.

A fondness for the bottle?

"The fellow never got fair-play. He would aye be

somewhere takin' a gless of something wi' somebody, for he's a fine big cheery chap." *[I/10]*

"Jeck had the duvvle's own bad luck: he couldna' take a gless by-ordinar' but the ship went wrong on him, and he lost wan job efter the other, but he wass never anything but the perfect gentleman." *[I/10]*

"I got hold of a couple of men I knew in the China tred and went for chust wan small wee glass...what happened efter that's a mystery, but I think I wass drugged." *(The Disappointment of Erchie's Niece [I/24])*

To the innkeeper, also the local undertaker, who thought Jack had come to order the hearse for the funeral of a man who'd had two glasses of an unusual and reputedly lethal tipple the previous night: "'Cream de Mong?' said Jack with genuine interest: 'If it's anything like that, I'll try it!' " *(The Bottle King [III/14])*

"A night wi' Jeck iss ass good ass a college education – you never saw such nerve!" *(Hurricane Jack [III/1])*

A short temper?

"A nicer man on a boat you wouldna' meet, if you didna' contradict him" *(Piracy in the Kyles [II/15])*.

Arguing with a Tarbert fisherman that a tortoise is not an insect, but a bird: "If it wassna the Sabbath evenin'......I would give you a lesson in natural history that would keep you studyin' in your bed for a day or two." *(Hurricane Jack's Luck-bird [III/7])*

Persuading Para to go "on the committee" – that is, help run the private bar – at the Knapdale Ball to which Jack plans to take his girl-of-the-moment Jean MacTaggart: "What I'm wantin' you on the committee for iss to keep me back from the committee room so that I'll not take a drop too much and affront the lassie. If you see me desperate on takin' more than would be dacent, take a dozen strong smert fellows in wi' you at my expense and barricade the door. I'll maybe talk aboot tearin' the hoose doon but, och, that'll only be my nonsense." *(The Disappointment of Erchie's Niece [I/24])*

And finally, as a natural lead to the next topic, there is the assessment of the man's character given by Dougie in the story of the "luck-bird" already quoted from: "If he wassna' puttin' the fear o' daith on his fellow-bein's, he wass lookin' aboot for people to give money to."

A reckless generosity?

"What money he had, he would spend like the wave of the sea" says Para in *The Complete Gentleman [II/9]* though Macphail rather spoils the compliment by adding "It didna' maitter whose money it was, either".

Para Handy counters with: "People like Jeck should never be oot of money, they distribute it with such taste."

In *Fog [II/17]* "We spent three days in Glasgow, and all oor money."

In *Hurricane Jack [III/17]* he "....dragged out a leather bag and poured a considerable quantity of silver coinage on the counter. 'Set her up again, sunny boy,' he said to the barman: 'and don't vast heavin' till this little pot o' money's earned.'"

In short, Jack was a drouth, a brawler and a spendthrift. But fun with it.

We have to agree with Para Handy's assessment that "any man that found himsel' in Hurricane's company would find the time slip by" *(The Blockade Runner [BP/88])*: a good man to have on your side, or at your back if it came to a fight, and a character so vivid that in many respects he comes across as a more rounded figure than even the skipper himself.

* * * * *

One last aspect of Hurricane Jack's personality remains to be briefly considered. His relations with the ladies.

He seems to be a highly successful womaniser, on the evidence of stories like *The Disappointment of Erchie's Niece [I/24]* or *Fog [II/17]* or *Leap Year on the Vital Spark [III/11]* or *A Double Life [III/25]*. Yet for all that, Para describes him in the Leap Year yarn as "never a gallanter man in oilskins, but he's tumid, tumid among women" and as "no' much o' a hand at flirtin' by word o' mooth". This strange contradiction in the characterisation of the man is hard to explain – in every other circumstance he is played up as something of a dandy and an accomplished conversationalist. The only explanation would seem to be that, for the purposes of that one story, Jack has to be shown as "blate" with the ladies: and Neil Munro takes a little liberty in altering an already established character for the purposes of the one tale.

A greater mystery is contained in the recently-discovered story about blockade running contained in the Birlinn Edition *[BP/88]*. In this story, Hurricane Jack bamboozles the Spanish revolutionaries who board his ship by passing off his marriage lines as some sort of official document.

Marriage lines? Nowhere else is it ever suggested that Jack is or has been married. Indeed he seems the epitome of the footloose and fancy free bachelor. What happened? In the final appendix to this volume, one possible theory is advanced in the course of a look at the new stories.

* * * * *

To come full circle and offer a few concluding thoughts on Para Handy's oldest and dearest friend, I stand by my earlier statement, that I believe that the Hurricane Jack we meet in the pages of the stories is very firmly based on somebody of Neil Munro's acquaintance. More: I think this was a *friend*.

There may be exaggerations in the way he is presented, there may be occasional discrepancies in the account of his career or in the manner in which he is characterised, but overall there is a very positive sense of the reality, the believability, and the consistency of the very nature of the man.

All Neil Munro's characters ring true but, surely, none more so than Hurricane Jack. He could not just have simply invented someone so full of life, so blessed with the gift of bringing pleasure to his friends and to everyone who meets him, yet so cursed with the inner frailties which will inevitably destroy him in the end.

This world is full of "Hurricane Jacks". Just who Neil Munro's was we shall never establish after all these years: but he set down for all time a vivid portrait of a very special sort of person.

How many do you know?

Appendices

—

CHAPTER 12

Cast of Characters

[——], ALICK
Cantankerous, suspicious and (when it suits him) "deaf"
uncle of Para Handy's bride – the widow Crawford *(q.v.)*
– who mellows (and also miraculously recovers his hearing) as soon as he realises that the engaged couple have
come to visit him to give him a present, and not to tap him
for a loan towards the costs of their wedding. *[I/25]*

[——], DONALD
Friend of Para Handy's who runs a highly profitable
"farm" of thirteen old age pensioners, all carefully se-
lected long-living MacLeans, at Loch Scridain on Mull.
Their State pensions – then a recent introduction – bring
in a total of £169 a year: they grow their own potatoes and
Donald buys bulk meal for them in Oban, showing a
handsome return on his "investment". *[II/2]*

[——], DAN
Tighnabruaich boat-hirer from whom Para Handy buys a
punt when the **Vital Spark**'s own boat is confiscated by
the police after being abandoned during a poaching esca-
pade. Para Handy thinks he's driven a hard bargain: but
Dan shows a useful profit over what he paid for the boat
three years previously. *[II/22]*

[—], FLORA
Flirtatious Duror barmaid who invites Sunny Jim – and in
particular his melodeon – to the Appin Leap Year Ball.
Para Handy and Dougie make sure that the only other
musician present on the night – a piper – is so well plied

with drink as to be incapable of producing a note. Thus Jim is kept playing throughout the dance while the skipper and mate enjoy Flora's company to themselves. *[III/13]*

[——], KATE
Laundrymaid to the Sheriff at Inveraray, put forward by Para Handy as a possible bridal candidate for the would-be uxorious Tar: the crew pay a call on her with "shattering" results. *[I/13]*

BONNIE ANN
Un-prepossessing dairy-cum-greengrocery proprietrix who conducts seances on the side. The crew visit her for news of Hurricane Jack, who has jumped ship after receiving a letter hinting at a Leap Year proposal from Mary Maclachlan *[1] (q.v.)*. What Jack had not realised was that the letter was a forgery produced by the crew themselves – but the joke backfired on them when Jack did a runner. *[III/12]*

CAMERON, CALUM
Campbeltown man, jilted just before his wedding, whose intended's superfluous wedding cake was displayed for sale by raffle in the window of the bakery owned by the widow Crawford *(q.v.)*. This led directly to Para Handy himself finally proposing to the widow and, eventually, tying the knot. *[I/25]*

CAMERON, [——]
Colintraive coal-merchant, and rival to a customer of Para Handy's, use of whose "inferior" wares the skipper blames for the toughness of a coal-fish which was passed off as a prime cod and sold to a (latterly) disgruntled Glasgow holidaymaker by Dougie the mate. *[I/19]*

CAMERON, LIZA
Tailor's daughter – home unspecified but probably somewhere on Loch Fyne – wooed by Sunny Jim in the early days of the First War. But he loses her to a soldier, is taunted by her for not enlisting himself, and in disgust decides to join the army. *[III/21]*

CAMERON, LUCY

Glasgow girlfriend of Hurricane Jack. His evening out with her to Hengler's Circus becomes a philanderer's nightmare when a young widow from Oban whom he is also courting arrives on his doorstep expecting to be taken to the Glasgow Mull and Iona Soirée, Concert and Ball – a "double booking" which had completely slipped his mind. For four hours he alternates between the two venues and the two ladies – and gets away with it. He is only caught out when the *Oban Times* prints the list of guests at the Mull and Iona event, with Hurricane Jack's name prominent. Lucy sees it: and a spiteful friend tells the Oban widow too – so Jack loses the affections of both of the ladies. *[III/25]*

CAMPBELL, [——]

Bank manager in Tarbert who is briefly referred to in *A Night Alarm*. *[I/16]*

CAMPBELL, DOUGALD

Better known as "Dougie". The long-suffering, amenable, rather gullible and somewhat hen-pecked mate of the **Vital Spark** seems resigned to his fate. Though usually led, rather than leading, he has his moments – and is the skipper's staunchest ally and affirmation of all his tales despite being a regular target for his derogatory comments and teasing pranks. His full name is not given till tale number 13 of the second series of stories. [See Chapter 10 : *The Crew]*

CAMPBELL, PETER

Bridegroom of Mary Maclachlan *[1] (q.v.)*, an Ardrishaig girl once somewhat bashfully courted by Hurricane Jack *[III/11]*

CAMPBELLS, [——]

Wee Free farming family from Clonary in Argyll, regular donors of white hares to the Tarbert policeman of the same religious persuasion. *[I/17]*

CARMICHAEL, JOHN

Glendaruel soldier, repatriated from the First War trenches

with shrapnel in his ankle, who is credited by Para Handy with introducing the secret weapon of a "gas attack" on the German front lines by frying up quantities of Lochboisdale Herring whenever the wind is from the west. *[BP/92]*

CARMICHAEL, PETER

Arran entrepreneur whose business Para Handy considers taking over: for a trial period the two work together, buying eggs from farms and crofts all round the island for re-sale in Glasgow – till the owner of the **Vital Spark** finds out what's going on, and then proceeds to pocket the entire profits for himself. *[II/7]*

CARR-GLYN [——]

Opposition parliamentary candidate in Para Handy's constituency whose canvasser gets the promise of the captain's vote, as does the sitting MP Harry Watt *(q.v.)*. *[III/26]*

CLEGHORN, SUSAN

Widow of a Tarbert baker, whose "interest" in local coal merchant Eddie MacVean *(q.v.)* is discreetly hinted at – though in fact completely invented – by Para Handy as part of his campaign to get MacVean's reluctant wife to agree to move to Lochgilphead, where her husband has been offered an excellent business opportunity. *[III/24]*

CRAWFORD, MARY

Campbeltown baker's widow whom Para Handy courts ineptly for some years – to the considerable amusement of the crew, from whom he thinks this "secret" is safe – and who eventually marries him and settles in Glasgow.

CRAWFORD, WULLIE

Mild-mannered and seemingly docile Tarbert policeman during Para Handy's schooldays in Kintyre who regularly takes on and successfully outwits the wildest and most lawless of all the Tarbert fishermen, John McVicar *(q.v.)*. *[II/25]*

DENOVAN, [——]

Brash and gold-festooned English confidence trickster whom the skipper and Dougie encounter in a Greenock pub, masquerading as an Admiralty official arranging housing for workers at the government torpedo-factory in Gourock. He promises to put Para Handy down for a house in an effort to persuade him to "trust" him with a five pound note – for a dare. *[II/24]*

DEVLIN [——]
Glasgow publican in whose premises Para Handy and the crew try to buy a beer – unsuccessfully, as Para had planned – after closing time. *[BP/91]*

DWIGHT [——]
Proprietor of a dairy in Plantation, Glasgow, patronised by the mate's family. *[I/20]*

FLOOD, JACK
Glasgow holidaymaker at Crarae who mistakes the **Vital Spark** for the Broomielaw steamer – which has sailed already. He persuades Para Handy to give himself, wife and two children accommodation in the fo'c'sle for the weekend. The crew find their lodgers much more trouble than they're worth – and have to resort to a ruse to get them off the boat on the Monday. In the process the skipper completely forgets to collect the lodgings money. *[I/8]*

GRANT, PETER
West Highland innkeeper and big-time speculator-in-glass known as the "Bottle King", to whom Hurricane Jack successfully sells back a quantity of his own bottles to fund a drinking spree for the crew. *[III/14]*

GRANT, REVEREND
Teetotal Minister who officiates at the Tar's wedding – and is then rapidly seen off the premises at the reception by Para Handy so that the festivities can start in earnest. *[I/18]*

GREEN, DAVIE
Deckhand of the **Vital Spark** in most of the stories. A cheerful prankster and practical joker, better known as "Sunny Jim", he is cousin to the "Tar", Colin Turner *(q.v.)* the original deckhand of the **Vital Spark.** Sunny Jim takes over soon after the Tar's wedding, making his debut in the

first story in the second series. [See Chapter 10: *The Crew]*

JENKINS, [——]
The "English gentleman" in charge of the guns in Para Handy's imaginary "Mystery Ship" adventures. Very much in cahoots with Hurricane Jack during these fictitious scrapes, and full of mischief and trickery. *[III/3, 4 and 5]*

KERR, COLIN
Young friend of Para Handy from Tarbert, serving in the Royal Navy aboard HMS **Formidable**. *[II/14]*

KERR, SANDY
Brodick canary-fancier with whom Para Handy makes a wager that he owns a superior singing bird. Kerr later reneges on the bet and agrees to pay up half the stake as a penalty – not realising that the bird which Para Handy bought to put up against his is in fact dead. *[I/2]*

MACALISTER, JOHN
Publican in whose premises. location not stated but perhaps in Arran, Para Handy meets the gullible Glasgow Fair holidaymakers who are treated to the "Mystery Ship" yarns. *[III/2]*

MACALPINE, [——]
Farmer in Catacol, Arran, from whose flock Hurricane Jack steals and kills a sheep, hiding it by tying the carcase to the anchor when the farmer and his shepherds – having witnessed the theft from a distance – come to search the boat. *[I/10]*

MACCALLUM, DUNCAN
Boat-hirer at an un-named Clyde resort whose stock of craft Para Handy maligns as "cogly" to an English visitor. *[BP/98]*

MACCALLUM, JOHN
Skipper-owner of the Tighnabruaich gabbart **Katharine-Anne** which is salvaged off Ettrick Bay by the **Vital Spark** after being abandoned by her crew in a storm. He

faces ruin – according to his wife and daughters – if Para Handy submits the claim for salvage to which he is entitled. *[II/6]*

MACCALLUM, LUCY

Campbeltown girl – "kind of dull in the hearing" – whom the Tar marries. Her widowed mother has her eye on Para Handy, who is not totally disinterested, at least till he finds out – through her own indiscreet reply to his questioning – that she has no inheritance. *[I/18]*

MACCALLUM, WILLIAM

Alcoholic Campbeltown carter, better known by his nickname of "The Twister". According to his distraught wife the last time he was sober was "the year they took the lifeboat over the Machrihanish" but Hurricane Jack puts him "on the wagon" for life in the classic story of the phantom horse and cart. This must rank as one of the funniest and most ingenious of all the Para Handy tales. *[III/6]*

MACCLURE, COLIN

Otherwise known as the "Wet Man of Muscadale", who spends the last forty years of his life – dying at ninety – in a state of permanent dampness. He lives in, on and under water, and drinks as much of it again, believing it to be the remedy for all of life's ills. *[III/26]*

MACDERMOTT, JOHN

Colonsay Innkeeper who advises a teetotal English tourist that a good dram of spirits is the best antidote to the infamous Colonsay midges. *[III/15]*

MACDIARMID [——]

Claddich innkeeper whose pub Para Handy almost buys at the time he contemplates giving up the sea for a shore job. *[II/7]*

MACDONALD, [——]

Highland "piper" whom Para Handy recruits – on the doorstep of a Loch Fyne pub – to play at the wedding of his cousin at Kilfinnan. He turns out to be a tinker who has stolen the pipes, on which he cannot play a note. *[I/14]*

MACDOUGALL, [——]
Tarbert Merchant and one of the town's few Wee Frees.
[I/17]

MACDOUGALL BROTHERS
Three Minard fishermen, hard-drinking and hard-fighting enemies of John McVicar, a.k.a. "The Goat": Constable Crawford sets up an encounter between them so that he can "pick up the pieces" of The Goat when the battle is over. *[II/25]*

MACDOUGALL, COL
Kilfinnan fisherman who buys the "lucky tortoise" which has brought Hurricane Jack such continuing good fortune at the fishings. The bargain is proceeded with despite the fact that the tortoise is now dead – or so they both think. Neither seems to have heard of hibernation..... *[III/7]*

MACDOUGALL, JOHN
Tarbert fishermen, acquaintance of Para Handy. Meeting a man in one of the local pubs Para believes him to be John. In fact it's his brother Peter, whom Para does not know, and he mischievously invites the crew to John's home for their dinner. *[III/19]*

MACDOUGALL, KATRIN
Wife of John. The crew of the **Vital Spark** arrive at her house unexpectedly for a meal – when her husband is away at the fishing – thanks to the practical joke perpetrated by his brother Peter (previous entry). *[III/19]*

MACDOUGALL, PETER
Brother – and double – of John (above). *[III/19]*

MACFADYEN, JOHN
A cousin of Dougie's wife, crofter in Kilbride, who is persuaded by the mate to pretend that he has three sons in the armed forces in order to counter the malicious tales of the cowardice of the Kilbride community which Dougie feels reflect on the character of his wife's family name. In fact, John has only one son – and he's an ironmonger in Airdrie. *[BP/87]*

MACFADYEN SISTERS
The shape of two large rocks on the seashore in the Kyles of Bute, which later will become world-famous as the "Maids of Bute", remind a MacBrayne skipper, under whom Para Handy once served, of these two sisters from Pennymore. When English tourists can't see the stones' resemblance to two women, the exasperated skipper puts Para Handy ashore to paint the rocks to make them look more life-like. A fictional embellishment of a factual story. The "Maids" did exist. *[II/19]*

MACFARLANE, [——]
Un-named cousin of Para Handy who runs a "Pension Farm" of five uncles on the island of Gigha. *[II/2]*

MACFARLANE, CHERLIE [1]
Brother of Para Handy: appears just once and then only by proxy, referred to in the "Wee Teeny" story as being the father of twins. *[I/4]*

MACFARLANE, CHERLIE [2]
93-year-old cousin of Para Handy, living in Dunmore, near Tarbert, from whom the skipper entertains "hopes" of an inheritance. *[II/5]*

MACFARLANE, DOUGALD
Kilfinnan cousin of Para Handy who asks him to find a piper to play at his wedding. This leads to Para Handy recruiting the man he meets carrying a set of bagpipes outside the Inn at Cairndow. *[I/14]*

MACFARLANE, PETER
"Para Handy". Raconteur and ringleader. The character of the skipper of the **Vital Spark** is strongly marked by contrast and contradiction. Soft-hearted and easy going, but possessed of a sharp tongue, he is generous – but acquisitive as well: shrewd in most situations, yet gullible in others. His greatest asset is his love of life, his most-entrenched attributes a fierce pride in his calling and a blind love for his ship. [See Chapter 9: *Who was Para Handy?*]

MACINTYRE, [——]
Loch Fyneside joiner/undertaker who is roped in to put paid to the Tar's malingering by pretending to measure him for his coffin as he lies "ill" in his bunk. *[I/3]*

MACKAY [——]
Glasgow policeman to whom the crew try to "turn in" a Basque onion-seller who has stowed away on the **Vital Spark**. Believing him to be a German spy they batten him down in the fo'c'sle and only when it is too late do they discover that while there he has stolen the mate's silver watch from his bunk. *[II/23]*

MACKAY, CORPORAL DAN
Wounded soldier who steals Liza Cameron's affections from Sunny Jim and leads to his attempt to enlist in the army. *[III/21]*

MACKAY, JOHN
Tarbert joiner and undertaker. *[III/24]*

MACKAY, LACHIE
Purser of the steamer **Texa** with whom Para Handy exchanges some lighthearted insults at Rothesay Pier when Sunny Jim arrives from Glasgow on that ship to join the Vital Spark. *[II/1]*

McKERRACHER, [——]
Alleged "victim" of Tarbert tearaway John McVicar, a.k.a. "The Goat", *(q.v.)*. *[II/25]*

MACKINLAY, MATHILDE VAVASOUR
One of the Land Girls on the Loch Fyne forestry plantation where the crew of the **Vital Spark** attend a Hallowe'en party with an unexpected climax. *[III/10]*

MACKINNON, [——]
Itinerant milkman in an un-named harbour, the bells of whose cart are blamed for Para Handy's 'mistake' in failing to give way to the ringing bells of the mail vessel. *[BP/90]*

MACLACHLAN [——]
Innkeeper at Lochgair on Lochfyneside from whom Para

Handy's "piper" (Macdonald, *q.v.*) tries to borrow a reed. MacLachlan is not a piper at all, it turns out: Para Handy's "piper" is just wanting ashore for a dram. *[I/14]*

MACLACHLAN, BELLA

Girl from Cowal, working as cook to a Glasgow household, who is for a while the object of Hurricane Jack's affections. A party in her employer's house, in his absence, turns into a disaster when Jack moves the household's piano downstairs – and Bella's employer returns home unexpectedly when his train is cancelled due to fog. *[II/17]*

MACLACHLAN, COL

Crarae quarryman whose widow sails on board the **Vital Spark** to Lochgilphead – destination the Poorhouse: until, that is, Para Handy explains her rights to a state pension. *[II/18]*

MACLACHLAN, JOHN

"Hurricane Jack": tearaway, philanderer, trickster, former deep-sea-man and Para Handy's dearest, oldest – and shamelessly hero-worshipped – friend. Jack has obviously come "down in the world" – having at one stage been a skipper in sail. But he bears no grudges, carries no chip, and brings the makings of a spree with him wherever he goes. He appears both as occasional crewman on the **Vital Spark,** and occasional visitor ashore and afloat. *[See Chapter 11: Hurricane Jack]*

MACLACHLAN, MARY (1)

Loch Fyne sweet-shop proprietor, object of the attentions of Hurricane Jack whose inarticulateness with women results in his carrying out most of the courting with conversation lozenges. *[III/11]*

MACLACHLAN, MARY (2)

See Maclachlan, Wilyum. *[III/28]*

MACLACHLAN, MRS

Wealthy Oban widow, assiduously but not exclusively courted by Hurricane Jack, who throws him over on discovering that he is two-timing her with Glasgow girl

Lucy Cameron *(q.v.)*. *[III/25]*

MACLACHLAN, WILYUM

Hurricane Jack's only male relative, a former market gardener aged 92, who is expected to leave his money to Jack. But he turns into a religious crank, believing that a second flood is coming. Wilyum's only other relative – his sister Mary – lives on Colonsay and Jack takes him to stay with her. The old man lingers there to the age of 99, quite convinced that every day will be the last day of the world, and then leaves everything to his sister in his will. *[III/28]*

MACLEAN, [——] Mrs

Salen, Mull, gamekeeper's wife from whom the crew buy eggs for profitable re-sale on the "Black Market" in Glasgow. Given a Commission by a Glasgow customer to get a pair of hens, Para Handy palms off two herons which he has acquired from Mrs MacLean: surprisingly, his client is not too unhappy with the deal, but she thinks the birds are ducks! *[BP/96]*

MACLEAN FAMILY

A Kenmore family, one of whom was the mother of the Vital Spark's engineer Dan Macphail. They are unflatteringly referred to by Para Handy in *A Night Alarm*. *[I/16]*

MACLEOD, COLIN

Minard fisherman and Freemason, friend of Para Handy, who persuades him that he should join the Tarbert Lodge – but that he will first need to have a suit appropriate for the occasion made by MacLeod's tailor cousin. Para Handy mistakenly goes to the wrong outfitter, and so winds up (briefly) in the Rechabites. So far as we know, the skipper never does become a Mason. *[III/27]*

MACLEOD, SERGEANT

Tarbert policeman who takes Para Handy into custody – though he releases him as soon as he finds out that both of them are Wee Frees – on the night the puffer's steam whistle wakes the whole town at two in the morning. *[I/16]*

MACMILLAN, [——]
Glasgow pawnbroker, briefly referred to with the insinuation that Dougie the mate is a regular client. *[I/20]*

MACMILLAN, MARY
Nominated to be the recipient of the rings of Liza McVean (*née* Walker) *(q.v.)* by their owner on her feigned "deathbed". *[III/24]*

MACNAB, [——]
One-eyed boatbuilder from whose yards came the gabbart **Sarah** on which Para Handy and Dougie sailed for six years before being appointed to the **Vital Spark**. One interpretation is that Para actually owned the gabbart. *[BP/83]*

MACNAIR [——]
Engineer of the **Julia**, puffer on which Para Handy sailed with Hurricane Jack at some point prior to taking up his command of the **Vital Spark** – but presumably before he was master of the **Sarah**. (See above). *[II/17]*

MACNAUGHTON, CONSTABLE
Village policeman in an unnamed location – possibly Carradale – who prevents the crew from "dumping" a scrap German cannon which Para Handy has bought from a hawker in Lochgilphead and can neither sell – nor get rid of it. Till his encounter with MacNaughton, though, Para Handy hadn't thought of the obvious solution – to pitch it overboard in Kilbrannan Sound. *[III/29]*

MACNEILL FAMILY
Distant relatives of Para Handy, and rival candidates for the legacy of his cousin Cherlie MacFarlane. *[II/5]*

MACPHAIL, DAN
Engineer of the **Vital Spark**. Pessimist, fatalist, occasional mysoginist, aficionado of penny dreadfuls. He is engaged in a permanent battle to keep his clapped-out engine turning and a semi-permanent war of words with the crew in general and Para Handy in particular. [See Chapter 10: *The Crew*]

MACPHAIL, JOHNNY
Dan's son – himself an apprentice engineer – who appears in the very last of the stories as the maker and installer of the puffer's very first wireless set. *[BP/99]*

McQUEEN, REV JOHN
West Highland minister whose church Para Handy and Dougie attend the morning after the clocks were put forward for Summertime by Sunny Jim and MacPhail on the instructions of the skipper. They find themselves arriving at Sunday School, not the service, because the time had been maliciously advanced three hours instead of one. *[III/118]*

MACRAE, [——]
The Glasgow policeman to whom Bella Maclachlan *(q.v.)* has become secretly engaged – unknown to the amorous Hurricane Jack. [II/17]

MACRAE, [——]
Captain of the passenger launch **Kate**, and a native of Gigha of whose antecedents Para Handy speaks disparagingly. By virtue of carrying the mails, the **Kate** is entitled to berthing priority which Para Handy denies Macrae at an un-named West Highland harbour. *[BP/90]*

MACRAE, REV GEORGE
Tarbert parish minister who persuades Col. MacDougall *(q.v.)* to sign the pledge when the "dead" tortoise he had bought from Hurricane Jack wakes up from its winter hibernation. *[III/7]*

MACRAE, MIMA
Arrochar woman of indeterminate age, occasionally courted by Dan MacPhail. In determination to hide his baldness, he has never taken his cap off in her presence. Since it is confirmed elsewhere in the stories that Dan is married this appears to be the only hint of marital infidelity anywhere in the stories. *[III/15]*

MACTAGGART, JEAN
Carradale girl, niece of Erchie Macpherson *[Erchie, My Droll Friend* – a Glasgow waiter and beadle, the epony-

mous subject of another series of Neil Munro stories] who is, though only briefly, affianced to Hurricane Jack. Erchie himself appears in the story. This is the only instance of cross-linking of Munro characters from different books. *[I/24]*.

MACTAVISH, JOHN
Crewman of the MacBrayne steamer **Cygnet**, miscalled by Para Handy (in a case of mistaken identity) in *A Lost Man. [I/9]*

MACVEAN, EDDIE
Tarbert carter and friend of Para Handy, whose wife refuses to move to Lochgilphead when he gets the offer of a good business in that town – but Para Handy gets the better of her and ensures that the move is made. See under Walker, Liza *[III/24]*

MCVICAR, JOHN
Better known as "The Goat". Heavy-drinking, hard-fighting and outrageously rampaging Tarbert fisherman in full flight at the height of the Loch Fyne herring boom, who was tamed by the wiles of the innocuous-looking local policeman Wullie Crawford *(q.v.)*. *[II/25]*

PODGER
Nickname of the otherwise unidentified harum-scarum daughter of a douce Midlothian manse who is one of the leading lights of the Loch Fyne Land Girls who help Hurricane Jack to win a bet by getting Dougie to wear a skirt. *[III/10]*

SINCLAIR, SANDY
Tarbert carter for whom the **Vital Spark** is delivering a cargo of coals in *A Night Alarm [I/16]*

SINCLAIR, PATRICK
Young Skye man who wins the "cheese" presented by Para Handy to the organisers of the ploughing match at Portree in one of the imaginary *Mystery Ship* stories. *[III/5]*

SLOAN, JERRY
Shipmate from Hurricane Jack's days on the clippers with
whom he tries (unsuccessfully) to go "out on the town" in
Glasgow at midnight. *[III/1]*

SMITH [———]
First owner of the **Vital Spark**, who makes a brief
retrospective appearance in the story about Para Handy's
business ventures on Arran. *[II/7]*. The second owner of
the puffer – though on occasion referred to and round
whose schoolboy son's desire to go to sea one entire
episode *[I/11]* is built – is never named.

STEVENSON, WILLIE
Glasgow riveter, by inference employed at Fairfield's
shipyard and from whom Sunny Jim borrows the disastrous, dangerous and deaf watchdog "Biler" after the
sneak-theft of the crew's alarm clock. *[II/3]*

TAYLOR [———]
Manager of the tree plantation on Loch Fyne where the
bemused crew of the **Vital Spark** encounter the totally
unexpected in the shape of the Land Girls. *[III/10]*

TURNER, COLIN
Better known as the "Tar": the puffer's first deck-hand.
He is rarely referred to by his christian name and only once
[I/23] by his surname. Laziness, untidiness, inability to
cook and a fondness for sleep at any time of the day or
night are his main qualities. All seems to change when he
leaves the puffer to work on a private yacht. *[II/11]* [See
Chapter 10: *The Crew]*

WALKER, LIZA
Maiden name of Eddie McVean's wife, who has taken to
her bed pretending to be at death's door in their Tarbert
home in order to stop him moving to take over a business
in Lochgilphead. But Para Handy gets her believing that
a Tarbert widow has her eye on her husband. She then
makes a miraculous recovery: and the move! *[III/24]*

WATT, HARRY
Sitting Member of Parliament for Para Handy's College Division constituency, whose canvasser calls seeking electoral support from the Captain. *[II/26]*

"WEE TEENY"
Three year old girl accidentally left behind at Ardrishaig by her mother (who thinks she's with her father) and father (who thinks she's with her mother) on the evening of Glasgow Fair Saturday. Given passage on the **Vital Spark** she catches up with her parents (and 10 brothers and sisters) at Rothesay, in the process winning the affection of the entire crew. *[I/4]*

WEIR, [——] Bailie
Luminary of the Marine Court before whom Para Handy is tried following the puffer's collision with the French cargo steamer **Dolores**. Verdict: not proven. Para Handy unsuccessfully tries to persuade the French skipper to join them in a celebratory dram. *[BP/84]*

WILSON, TOM
Pretended blue-water sailor, but in fact the foil and side-kick of the English con-man Denovan *(q.v.),* who tries to "set-up" Para Handy for a patsy in a Greenock pub. *[II/24]*

Chapter 13

What happened where

Neil Munro identifies the setting for many of the stories and episodes in the Para Handy tales. Harbours and communities which he knew well feature regularly as the factual locations for the fictional happenings.

It is not surprising that Loch Fyne side, where his own roots lay, is often used as the backdrop for the stories and in many other cases, even where the actual location is not named, there is evidence enough to infer that he had the area very much in mind when he was writing.

Dozens of other harbours and communities are featured as well, however, and anyone familiar with the tales can indulge in an imaginative daydream when visiting these places, recognising that such-and-such an event happened "right here" and enjoying the illusion of picturing exactly what happened.......

ARDLAMONT

Here, where the Kyles of Bute open out into the foot of Loch Fyne, Ardlamont Point has been a prominent seamark for decades and was a measure of a vessel's progress whether outward or homeward bound.

In some respects it also marks the transition from the Inner to the Outer Firth. As Para Handy records, if the **Vital Spark** was lying on Saturday mornings at any pier "inside Ardlamont" then Dougie's wife would be down on the first steamer from Glasgow to take his wages off him before he could spend them.

It was rounding Ardlamont in heavy weather, Rothesay-bound, that the puffer chanced on John McCallum's abandoned gabbart **Katharine-Anne** drifting derelict, and, securing a line on board her, towed her safely to her home port at Tighnabruaich.

ARDRISHAIG

This Loch Fyne harbour was the staging post for passengers and freight bound for the further reaches of the Western and Northern Highlands and MacBrayne's maintained their Gourock to Ardrishaig service until 1969.

The **Vital Spark** was much in and around the village. Here, "Wee Teeny" was inadvertently left behind by her parents and taken on to Rothesay by the besotted crew of the puffer. *[I/4]* It was at the Inns at Ardrishaig that Para Handy met up with The Tar the morning after he sacked him following a quarrel at the Furnace Ball – though alcohol-induced amnesia meant he remembered nothing at all about it. *[I/9]* And it was at the same Inns that Para Handy's tinker "piper" finally did a bunk with the pipes he'd stolen from Cairndow. *[I/14]*

ARROCHAR

This picturesque village at the head of Loch Long is still as notorious for its midges as it was in Para Handy's time, though modern repellents keep the monsters at bay rather more effectively than the syrup the crew persuaded Dan Macphail to smear all over his face when he went ashore to visit Mima Macrae *[III/15]*. As Para put it, "....she'll think it's no an enchineer she has to caal on her, but a fly cemetery".

BOWLING

This community grew up around the western end of the Forth and Clyde Canal, and was important as a transshipment point for goods and passengers from the Firth to the Canal. Many vessels, including the puffers themselves, regularly plied the canal with cargoes. The largest of all the puffer fleets – that of Hays of Kirkintilloch – started life as a canal-based service and many of the Clyde puffers were actually built at Kirkintilloch and launched sideways into the canal.

The **Vital Spark** is often described as being on passage to or from Bowling, and often lay there overnight or at weekends. It was here *[I/24]* that the scheming Hurricane Jack "treated Para Handy to three substantial refreshments in an incredibly short space of time" in the course of persuading him to join him at the Knapdale Natives' Ball in Glasgow.

BRODICK

The capital of the Island of Arran remains a busy harbour today as the pierhead for the crucial lifeline of the ro-ro service from Ardrossan.

Vital Spark was a regular visitor to the island. It was at Brodick that Para Handy accepted the challenge to produce a better songster than Sandy Kerr's canary "Wee Free" *[I/2]*, and here too that the crew's complaints about the monotony of the Tar's cooking led him to steal two chickens from the stern "pantry" of a moored cutter-yacht in the middle of the night, much to their consternation. *[I/7]*

BUNESSAN

The harbours of the island of Mull were other regular ports of call for Para Handy and his crew, but only one visit to the village of Bunessan is recorded. It was here *[III/8]* that Hurricane Jack was sent ashore to buy butter and, the local shop having none, came back instead with the goat stolen from an Irish goatherd.

However, the most intriguing aspect of the reference to this trip to Bunessan is what Neil Munro does *not* tell us. Hurricane Jack is sent ashore because he has never been there before, whereas the other members of the crew didn't dare show their faces in Bunessan "because of the deplorable incident of the minister's hens, when Para Handy and his men had to fight their way to their vessel through an infuriated populace."

What a tantalising reference to an otherwise unrecorded fracas which, even by the high standards of the

Vital Spark, must have been something really special.....

CAIRNDOW

Lying at the head of Loch Fyne, this tiny village – which has a particularly attractive and unusual, octagonal church – had a steamer pier, but it was probably while beached here that **Vital Spark** loaded with cargoes of oak bark or timber, and the crew encountered the emancipated Land Girls who so unnerved Dougie, at least. *[III/10]*. Certainly, it was at Cairndow that Para Handy recruited the "piper" for his cousin's wedding, not realising that the man was a tinker who'd been asked to hold onto the pipes for their owner, who was in the Inns having a dram. The puffer's progress down Loch Fyne thereafter was punctuated by the frequent and ill-disguised "refreshment stops" demanded by the bearer of the pipes.

CAMPBELTOWN

Scotland's most isolated mainland town, set at the tip of the long Kintyre peninsula, Campbeltown in Para Handy's time could only be reached comfortably by boat. The alternative to a surprisingly rapid sea passage (the fastest of the paddlers could make a return trip to Campbeltown from Glasgow in a day) was a tortuous road journey up Loch Lomond, across the Rest-and-be-Thankful to Loch Fyne, and south by way of Inveraray, Ardrishaig and Tarbert – a distance of nearly 140 miles.

The Tar was married in Campbeltown, as was Para Handy himself after six years of inept and surreptitious courting of the widow Crawford. Here they unsuccessfully tried to raise a collection for Sunny Jim's "swim" down Kilbrannan Sound, *[II/21]* and it was in Campbeltown harbour that the yacht Dolphin berthed and one of her deckhands turned out to be the Tar, who paid a visit to his old crewmates *[II/11]* though it's doubtful if he endeared himself to Para when he commented that "I knew the tarry old hooker ass soon ass I saw her at the quay".

The splendid tale of the drunken carter Twister McCallum and how Hurricane Jack turned him into a teetotaller overnight with the Phantom Horse and Cart was also set in Campbeltown *[III/6]*. And, like Bunessan [above] it also has tantalising secrets which Munro did not divulge! When the skipper is summoned to the owner's office *[Para Handy's Apprentice, I/11]* he confides to the crew that this must be either about a rise in pay – or else "he's heard aboot the night we had in Campbeltown."

Even that far from Glasgow, it seems, the news of the exploits of the **Vital Spark** and her crew could come back to haunt them!

CASTLEBAY

The capital of the southern Hebridean island of Barra must have claim to be the most beautiful harbour in the whole of the west of Scotland.

It's also the place where, for some reason or other, the otherwise usually docile Dougie renounced his Dr Jekyll nature and assumed the guise of Mr Hyde. After several encounters with Dougie on a monumental bender, the merchants of Castlebay agreed that the simplest solution was to shut up shop whenever the **Vital Spark** was seen approaching Castlebay pier. *[I/17]*

COLINTRAIVE

This village on the Argyll shoreline at the narrowest part of the Kyles of Bute was a popular port-of-call for the steamers and a favourite resort with many Glaswegians.

It was at Colintraive that Dougie succeeded in passing off a coal-fish as a cod to a Glasgow holiday-maker: the Tar was sent up to the Inns with a canister to buy beer with the proceeds of the sale. Para Handy's only disappointment with the mate was that he could have got twice as much money (and so beer) if he had pretended the fish was a salmon.

There was further deception at Colintraive when Sunny Jim told the owner of the borrowed watchdog "Biler" that the animal had been accidentally drowned here. *[II/3]*

CRARAE

Here, midway between Inveraray and Lochgoilhead, the crew made their one venture as landlords when they gave the stranded Flood family weekend accommodation aboard the puffer *[I/8]* and from Crarae Para Handy gave passage to Lochgilphead to Col. MacLachlan's widow, en route to the poorhouse because she did not realise, till the skipper told her, that she was entitled to a state pension and could therefore go back home and live an independent old age. *[II/18]*

DUROR

In Appin to load timber, the crew were persuaded to attend the Leap Year Ball and Sunny Jim, fallen under the spell of a local beauty, agreed to play his melodeon as "relief" to the piper engaged officially to provide the music at the event.

"That's a charming gyurl, and a desperate sober piper," said Para Handy: and ensured that enough drink was plied to knock the piper off his feet so that he and Dougie could spend the night dancing with Jim's girl, and to Jim's music. *[III/13]*

FURNACE

Back on Loch Fyne, the **Vital Spark** would presumably have made many trips to the renowned granite quarries at Furnace but only one is recorded – the occasion when the skipper quarrels with the Tar at a ceilidh and sacks him. But when the alcohol clears the next morning he can't remember a thing about it. *[I/9]*

GARELOCH

The innermost of all the Clyde estuary lochs was frequently used for mooring laid-up or redundant ships, and here Hurricane Jack spent a year in a "dream job" as caretaker aboard the barquentine **Jean and Mary**. In summer, he let out lodgings and in the winter she was available for parties and even a wedding, until the owner unexpectedly showed up and caught the unfortunate entrepreneur red-handed.

GOUROCK

The only two occasions on which Para is recorded as being in Gourock were when he had to find a dock in an emergency.

The first time, on the puffer Julia which he and Hurricane Jack crewed before he was appointed to the **Vital Spark** *[II/17]* was to escape a pea-soup fog. Unfortunately, he and Jack had been bidden to a party in Glasgow that night – so they left the **Julia** in charge of the engineer, and went up by train. Even more unfortunately, the party lasted three days and when it was over they couldn't remember where they'd left the boat, until they found a rail ticket stub in Jack's pocket.......

The second occasion involved the **Vital Spark**, which put in to shelter from a severe storm. Para Handy went up to Glasgow by train again, and was so carried away by his own stories of the storm, and the bottle freely passed by sympathetic travellers, that by the time the train reached Glasgow he had convinced them – and himself – that the puffer had been lost at sea.

GREENOCK

Gourock's neighbouring town was a major port for both coastal and sea-going craft in Para Handy's days, and the very first appearance of the **Vital Spark** in print *[I/1]* was set there. The crew had "gone on the skite" the day after New Year and the upshot was that they were all sacked following several days of belated celebration during which they ignored telegrams from the owner of their cargo, and drank the passage money which he gave them: but, thankfully for all the future fans of the puffer and her crew, they were reinstated the following week!

Later, it was in a Greenock pub that Para Handy and the mate met the English con-man Denovan and and his "straight man" Tom Wilson. *[II/24]*

INNELLAN

It was at Innellan pier that Dougie's wife disembarked from the Glasgow steamer the week following their wedding, in search of the mate's wages. All the crew joined him in sucking peppermint sweeties (their cargo, according to Para Handy – "six tons of them for the Tarbert fishermen") so that she wouldn't smell the dram on his breath.

INVERARAY

Given that it was Neil Munro's native town, it is surprising that there is only one specific mention of this historic burgh, when Para Handy and the mate go in search of a potential bride for the Tar. *[I/13]* Their objective is the laundrymaid at the Sheriff's house but when they discover she is away from home they try to recruit the matronly cook instead. Or, as Para puts it to the Tar, "It's no' the laundry-maid, but it's a far bigger one!"

However, many of the stories with unspecified Loch Fyne settings can almost certainly be placed in Inveraray.

These include recruiting the local undertaker to measure the malingering Tar for a coffin *[I/3]:* being forced to abandon the ship's boat on a poaching expedition *[I/6]:* the encounter with the medium Bonnie Ann *[III/12]:* and Para Handy's brief experiment with total abstinence and the crew's angry reaction to it. *[I/22]*

KILBRANNAN SOUND

The spectacular stretch of water which lies between the isle of Arran and the Kintyre peninsula can give a rough passage at times to boats the size of a puffer, but can equally be a sheet of tranquil blue.

It was the setting for Sunny Jim's spurious swimming marathon from Skipness to Campbeltown – an unsuccessful ploy to raise beer money for the crew in a summer heatwave. And it was the watery grave of the unfortunate parrot, part of a "flitting" cargo, whose mockery of the skipper's singing was just too much for the infuriated Para Handy. "If he says another word I'll throw him over the side". He did – and *he* did, too!

KILCATRINE

A tiny Loch Fyne hamlet, immediately across the water from Inveraray, from which the **Vital Spark** sailed with a badly trimmed cargo of oak bark. When they hit bad weather, the terrified Dougie persuaded Para Handy to put into Furnace for shelter on the occasion of the annual Furnace Ball. *[I/9]*

LOCHGILPHEAD

So shallow and silted is Loch Gilp that there has never been a steamer pier here, though the town is the largest in this part of mid-Argyll. Steamers berthed at Ardrishaig, a couple of miles south: and Ardrishaig was also the access point to the Crinan canal, which then ran north and skirted Lochgilphead before turning west to the Atlantic coast.

But it was in Lochgilphead that Para Handy unwisely invested in a scrap German cannon *[III/29]* offered for sale by a tinker.

Efforts to sell it at Cairndow for £1, at Strachur for 10/-, at Crarae for 1/-, all failed. They tried (unsuccessfully) to abandon it at Crarae, and finished up dumping it overboard in Kilbrannan Sound.

LOCHGOILHEAD

It was while berthed at this beautiful, isolated village that Para Handy attended a nearby farm sale and finished up buying a cow *[I/15]:* and it was here, one year, that the crew spent several days giving the puffer her annual "spring-clean" and then teased Para Handy into planning a career for her as a passenger steamer because she was much too smart a vessel to be carrying rubbishy cargoes. *[III/17]*

LOCHRANZA

The **Vital Spark** lay for a week in this little harbour on the west coast of Arran when the owner (her first owner) had quite forgotten where she was. Para Handy judiciously filled in the time by doing a little dealing in eggs. *[II/7]* On another visit to the harbour, a stowaway sneaked on board – a Basque onion-seller whom the crew suspected of being a German spy. *[II/23]*

And it was from the nearby farm at Catacol that Hurricane Jack "stole the sheep" and by so doing – though only Para Handy seems to have been capable of understanding precisely why – he earned his nickname.

LONDONDERRY

Para Handy records with pride that the **Vital Spark** made one trip to the Northern Ireland port, her one and only sortie outwith Scottish waters, on an overnight trip with no oil for the navigation lamps. Dougie sat in her bows and struck matches all the way across. *[I/1]*

ORMIDALE

As the puffer lay alongside this remote pier in beautiful Loch Ridden on a hot summer's afternoon, with a day and a half of idle time ahead, Para Handy tried to get the crew to turn to and do some painting and refurbishing. The result was probably the only "strike" ever to take place in that peaceful part of the world! *[II/7]*

ORONSAY

En route back to the Clyde with the ill-tempered goat which Hurricane Jack had stolen at Bunessan on board, they put in to this tiny and all but deserted island off the south coast of Colonsay to forage for fodder for their unwilling passenger. *[III/9]*

PORT ELLEN

It was at Islay's largest town that someone broke into the fo'c'sle of the **Vital Spark** and stole the ship's only clock while the crew were ashore at a shinty concert. *[II/3]*

Some years later, they finally managed to rid themselves of the hell-raising Bunessan goat at Port Ellen after it ran amok and forced the shopkeepers to put their shutters up. One was too late in doing so and the goat invaded the premises, staying put when it discovered that a supply of its favourite peppermint sweeties was to be had there.

As Para Handy put it, "Take oot the chart and score oot Port Ellen – that's another place we daurna enter in the Western Isles".

ROTHESAY

The **Vital Spark** seems to have made fewer calls at Rothesay than one might have expected, though she must have passed the capital of Bute on innumerable occasions as she plied to and from the harbours of Loch Fyne. But it was to Rothesay that the puffer brought Wee Teeny to be reunited with her parents *[I/4]* and where Sunny Jim, the Tar's replacement as deckhand, cook and bottlewasher, first joined the crew. *[II/1]*

And it was to a Rothesay photographers that the mate was taken ashore, togged out in the captain's best-and-only pea jacket, to have his picture taken as an essential ingredient of the crew's unsuccessful "Petroloid" hair-restorer scam. *[II/13]*

SKIPNESS

With the puffer berthed overnight at this isolated Kintyre pier shortly after the acquisition of the unprepossessing but effective watchdog "Biler", Para Handy went ashore to a party in his glad rags. On his return in the small hours, the dog didn't recognise the skipper out of his working clothes, and refused to let him set foot on deck. *[II/3]*

It was also from Skipness that Sunny Jim set off on his great Kilbrannan Sound swim – to the total apathy of the local populace. *[II/21]*

TARBERT

The Tarbert isthmus was the hub for much of the passenger and freight traffic on the Clyde in Para's days. The Loch Fyne port was a major fishing centre: on the other side of the narrow isthmus the steamers sailed with cargo (and tourists as well as residents) for Islay, Jura and Gigha.

It's not surprising therefore that the **Vital Spark** and her crew were frequently in and around Tarbert.

Here the skipper, mate and engineer held a protest meeting about the Tar's appalling catering standards while he was ashore to buy bottled coffee and corned beef in bulk. *[I/7]*

One of the puffer's more unusual cargoes was the "Shows", that is the stalls and their operators, which she carried to the fair at Tarbert. This was the occasion when Dougie was hypnotized by the Mesmeriser and "married" in front of the delighted crowd to the Fattest Woman in the

World. *[I/12]*

Other episodes at Tarbert included the arrest of Para Handy on the occasion when the puffer's steam whistle went off in the middle of the night and nobody would get out of bed to turn it off *[I/16]*: the purchase by the crew of the "mock" Valentine for the skipper, a prank which backfired on them when it was delivered in a mourning envelope and Para Handy took a day off by pretending he'd been bidden to a funeral *[I/23]*: the visit paid by skipper and mate to the same fortune teller, who gave them both the same reading with alarming and disconcerting results *[II/12]*.

During Para Handy's schooldays at Tarbert, the innocuous local "bobbie" Wully Crawford took on and tamed the fighting-drunk fisherman John McVicar, better known as "The Goat". *[II/25]*

The tale of Hurricane Jack's "lucky tortoise" and its influence on the Tarbert fishings *[III/1]*, Para Handy's scheming to help John MacDougall persuade his wife to move to Lochgilphead *[III/24]*, and the skipper's inadvertent recruitment into the Rechabites instead of the Masons, were also all set in the town and Neil Munro probably had Tarbert in mind as the site of many other tales where the exact location was not actually identified. Loch Fyne was his home territory after all, and it was only to be expected that much of the action would be set there.

What can only be speculated on at this distance is just how far some of the "shore-based" characters in the tales – such as the aforesaid John McVicar, or the alcoholic Campbeltown carter McCallum, or the con-man Denovan, were based on real people whom Munro knew, or knew of.

TIGHNABRUAICH

Best known of all the Kyles of Bute communities, Tighnabruaich was – and indeed still is, on the occasions of the summer visits to the Clyde of the paddle steamer Waverley – one of the most popular destinations for excursions "doon the watter".

Again, it was a harbour which the puffer would have visited many times in the course of her career. All Loch Fyne traffic passed through the Kyles both outward and inward bound.

It was to Tighnabruaich, her home port, that the abandoned gabbart **Katharine-Anne** was towed after Para and his crew had salvaged the boat off Ardlamont Point. *[II/6]*

In earlier years Hurricane Jack, over the course of a number of overnight berthings by the puffer **Aggie** on which he and Para Handy were then crewing, systematically stripped the small steam yacht **Eagle**, owned by an absentee Glasgow businessman, of virtually everything of value on her and in her. *[II/15]*

Even earlier than that, Para Handy rowed across to Bute from Tighnabruaich to paint the rocks known as the "Maids of Bute" on the instructions of the MacBrayne skipper under whom he was serving on the **Inveraray Castle**. *[II/19]*

Finally, it was a Tighnabruaich boat-hirer who sold Para Handy a rowing-boat to replace the one the puffer's crew had had to abandon when pursued by the water bailiffs during one of their regular poaching adventures. *[II/22]* Para Handy thought he had "done" the hirer: in fact, the hirer had "done" the skipper.

TOBERMORY

It was on Calve Island, separating Tobermory harbour from the Sound of Mull, that the crew saw a stranded whale and embarked on one of their few successful money-making operations by screening the carcase with canvas, charging holidaymakers for admission at the height of the Glasgow Fair Fortnight. *[II/4]*

And from Tobermory beach the unsuspecting captain took back some special "chuckie stanes" for his wife to make vegetarian soup from – unaware that he'd been duped by Sunny Jim. *[II/8]*

ULLAPOOL

To establish his credentials as no mere estuary sailor, Para

Handy cites his two trips to Ullapool, on the far north west coast of Ross-shire. Certainly these passages must have been the longest and farthest ever made by the **Vital Spark**. *[I/9]*

CHAPTER 14

Glossary

Throughout the stories there are references to land marks or events or organisations, people or places or things, which may not be familiar today to readers unacquainted with either the topography of the West of Scotland or the social history of the period in which the tales are set.

Here are notes on some of them. So brief and simple a glossary cannot cover them all, but it is hoped that many of the more intriguing, interesting or just plain incomprehensible have been covered!

AILSA CRAIG *[III/25]*
Otherwise known, and often referred to, as Paddy's Milestone. The Craig is an isolated granite rock, just three-quarters of a mile long but nearly 1200 feet in height, lying south of the island of Arran some ten miles west of the Ayrshire port of Girvan. The rock stands sentinel at the entrance to the Firth and its lighthouse was a welcome sight for homeward bound vessels. The **Vital Spark** would have been among them on her return trip from Londonderry.

The rock supports a large gannet colony and, in more practical matters, was quarried for many years for its much-reputed fine granite. Its main use was in the manufacture of curling stones and for many years no self-respecting curler would have played the "roaring game" with anything other than Ailsa stones.

BEARDMORES *[III/2]*

Long-established engineering and steelmaking company which moved into shipbuilding at the turn of the century, and to a new purpose-built yard at Renfrew in 1908. Beardmores had a particular reputation for warships, and many naval vessels were built for both British and foreign governments.

BLACK BALL LINE *[III/1]*

Atlantic passenger traffic was dominated for sixty years by this New York sailing packet company , the very first of the scheduled Transatlantic carriers, founded in 1816. Hurricane Jack was said to have served with the line: if so, he would have been well and truly kept on his toes. The Line had an unenviable reputation for brutal discipline and belligerent officers which helped it achieve the record-breaking passages for which it was renowned, and which ensured that it was patronised by the wealthiest travellers of the era.

Black Ball's monthly service between New York and Liverpool soon became bi-monthly, then tri-monthly as demand escalated and new ships were launched. The company's growing fleet of top-rated vessels were immediately recognisable at sea by the huge black ball painted (or sewn in contrasting canvas) onto the main fore topsails of the fleet.

By the early eighteen eighties, in common with virtually all transatlantic sail services, the Black Ball Line was forced into liquidation by the competition from the steamer fleets of Samuel Cunard and his contemporaries and rivals.

BLAVATSKY, MADAM *[III/12]*

One of the Victorian era's most vivid "characters" she was born Helena Hahn in Southern Russia in 1831. Married off at 16 to a much older man, she soon ran away and spent some years (among other occupations) as a circus bare-back rider, a magician, a piano tutor and a florist. She

surfaced in America in the eighteen seventies as a spiritu-
alist and founded the Theosophist Movement. She gained
worldwide fame as a "miracle worker" and author on the
occult – but the British Society for Psychical Research
exposed her as "one of the most accomplished, ingenious
and interesting impostors of history". She died in 1891.

BOOM *[BP 91]*
In both Wars the Clyde was a vitally important naval base,
and the assembly point for transatlantic convoys, many of
which in the Second War were of quite enormous size and
the spectacle of a convoy materialising from the anchorages of Gareloch and the waters at the Tail of the Bank
could last for hours as the ships put out to sea – in single
file at that stage with their destroyer escorts. In order to
guard against underwater attack on the anchored ships,
anti-submarine netting was suspended from a huge "boom"
which ran from the Cloch Lighthouse on the Renfrewshire
coast to Dunoon on the opposite shore of the firth. The
structure was attended by purpose-built boom-defence
vessels which could open and close the central "gate" to
allow Allied shipping in and out.

BOWL MONEY *[I/18]*
Originally, many decades previously, "Ball-money" – a
payment claimed from a wedding party to provide a ball,
or bowls, for the community in which the marriage took
place. By this time it meant simply the money which was
by tradition distributed to young folk assembled at the
spot where a marriage took place.

CHRISTY MINSTRELS *[III/17]*
George Christy, a New York theatrical impresario, introduced a troupe of white singing entertainers masquerading – boot-blacked faces, phoney southern accents and all
– as negroes as early as the mid-Victorian era. The
package remained a popular feature of seaside and music-
hall entertainment for decades and was even revived,

able as the concept would be today, as a popular BBC television programme just thirty years ago.

CLAN LINE *[BP 85]*

Clyde-based company, one of the largest of the many successful Scottish-owned shipping companies. All vessels in the fleet were named for Scottish Clans.

CONVERSATION LOZENGES *[III/11]*

Pressed fondant sweetmeats, tablets shaped in rectangular or oval, square or round and coloured white or pale pastels, which were embossed with messages which the tongue-tied lovelorn were intended to pass to the object of their desires. "Let us be always together": "You are the only one for me": "Can we ever be one?": "My heart is yours". These give just a flavour of the banality of the available vocabulary. Though it is possible to see how someone as inarticulate as The Tar might need to make use of such artificial aids to courting, they have usually always been seen as a joke rather than as the means for a serious attempt at wooing!

CLUTHAS *[II/1]*

The fast, smart little passenger steamers which provided an up and down river service within the city of Glasgow for about twenty years from the mid-eighties to the turn of the century. They were built to compete with the horse-drawn tram service already in operation, and did so so successfully, both in terms of comfort and cost (the go-anywhere fare on the Cluthas was just one penny) that the horse-trams were largely forced out of business. In the highly competitive public transport world of the day, however, the Cluthas themselves were in turn sent to the wall with the introduction of the electric tram.

COAL REE *[I/19]*

From the verb to "ree", or wall in – hence a coal-merchant's stockyard: Para Handy rarely misses the opportunity of a jibe at Dan Macphail and the suggestion is that the engineer was apprenticed to a trader in coal, rather than an engineering workshop.

CRACKERJACK *[II/24]*
A "savoury" dish concocted for clipper crews. Salt pork and ship's biscuit were mashed up in a shallow metal dish and baked in the galley oven to provide a hot evening meal.

DANDYFUNK *[II/24]*
Food on the clippers was notoriously inedible and generally unappetising: one of the few "delicacies" to which Hurricane Jack could have looked forward in his days on the Cape Horn passage was this grim-sounding mixture of ship's biscuit, fat and raw molasses mixed together and baked in a tray.

DEMURRAGE *[I/15]*
This is the payment which must be made by the owner of the cargo to compensate the ship-owner whom he has contracted to carry it in the event of any undue hold up in the delivery and loading of it which delays sailing time.

DREADNOUGHT *[II/14]*
This was the given name of one particular battleship, launched in 1906 from Portsmouth Dockyard in 1906. More importantly in naval terminology, however, was that the name came to be used to define the whole new generation of capital ships which followed her. The navies, not just of Great Britain but of the world, were classified at the time of the outbreak of the First War as deploying vessels falling into the categories of either *pre-* or *post-* Dreadnought.

The difference was not one of sheer size. Larger vessels were launched before that artificial "cut-off" date, smaller ones thereafter. What distinguished battleships designated as belonging to the Dreadnought class, what signified the way in which the ship of that name had broken the established mould, was the scale of their armaments. **Dreadnought** was the first capital ship to be armed solely with big guns: she was also, though this was not a prerequisite of Dreadnought status, the first to be solely reliant on the new turbine power which had been developed so swiftly and demonstrated so dramatically by the Parsons combine.

The original **Dreadnought** was a ship of some 18,000 tons, 530 ft. overall and with a crew of almost 800. Ironically, although she ushered in the new age of destructive capability at sea, she herself was never engaged in battle and was sold and broken up for scrap in 1923.

FAST DAYS *[I/6]*
Particularly in the Highlands, and above all in the rigorous dogmas of some of the splinter groups from the mainstream Church of Scotland, the week leading up to the Sunday which saw the celebration of the Lord's Supper was punctuated by preparatory services and the observance of self-denying "Fast Days". By the end of the last century the practice was in decline and backsliders like Para Handy were quite happy to turn the observance to their own advantage!

GABBART *[I/1]*
Scottish sailing coaster, about the same size as a puffer, from which the little steam ships were derived – and which they then put out of business.

GERMAN BAND *[I/5]*
In the closing years of the last century itinerant street musicians, originally from Germany but soon impersonated and overwhelmed by local imitators – the miniature equivalents of what we might today term an "oomph-pa" band – were often seen in British towns in summer months. They found their way on to the steamers too,

usually performing unpaid by the owners and relying for their livelihood on what they could collect from the passengers whom they entertained.

Though, needless to say, the designation of these performers as *German* bands did not survive the First War, let alone the Second, such ship-borne and usually freelance entertainment was still a feature of the Clyde steamers till their very last days in the nineteen sixties.

HENGLER'S CIRCUS *[III/25]*
This family dynasty was the nineteenth century equivalent of, say, Billy Smart or Bertram Mills. The first Hengler circuses dated from the end of the eighteenth century and by the beginning of the twentieth they had permanent shows in several of the largest industrial cities as well as an itinerant network of smaller packages. They would soon, like the music halls, become victims of the mass entertainment provided by the new technologies.

HINDENBURG LINE *[III/29]*
German fortified defences on the Western Front during the First War, named for General Paul von Hindenburg, later (after the war) to be elected President of the German Republic.

JUMPIN'-JECK *[I/4]*
What must surely have been one of the first toys to amuse a child ever created was bought by the crew to entertain "Wee Teeny" en route to Rothesay. Though by then manufactured out of card or wood, the Jumping Jack was originally made from the wishbone of a fowl, with a double cord looped across the two "arms" and a stick passed between them and twisted round to achieve torsion and spring. The sort of "toy", in other words, which one can well imagine Stone Age children playing with!

KEELIVINE *[BP/84]*
Almost everyone knows that "keelivine", and its several

variant spellings, was the old Scots word for a lead pencil. It's only worth mentioning here because nobody seems to know the actual derivation of the word: it would be very satisfying if someone could provide the answer to that unimportant but nevertheless intriguing etymological mystery.......

LAND O' HOUSES
In the West of Scotland dialect of the time, a "land" was any house with three or more storeys. By extension, a "land of houses" came to mean a tenement block. Tenements could be of any size from a simple, single block, to an entire street-length. They were usually of three, four or five storeys with the individual flats reached by way of a common "close" or passageway leading to a staircase which climbed the stairwell in the centre of the building. Though many became slums and have long since been demolished, others were handsome and well-located buildings and have been modernised and upgraded and still retain popularity today. The better ones were of red sandstone: the best boasted a "wally" or "china" close – one in which the common passageways and stair walls were lined with ceramic tiles!

LANGTRY, LILY *[II/13]*
Jersey-born Victorian actress, daughter of a manse, who later became mistress of the Prince of Wales, the future King Edward VII. She was famed more for her beauty and her social charms than for her acting abilities. Also known as the "Jersey Lily" from the title of her portrait painted by Sir John Millais.

NECROPOLIS *[I/22]*
From the cheery Greek word for "City of the Dead" this is the name for what was in Para Handy's time, and in many respects still is today, the most prestigious of all of Glasgow's many cemeteries. Adjacent to St Mungo's Cathedral, it has been the favoured resting place of the

city's would-be great and hopefully-good for more than a century and a half. The elaborate Victorian and Edwardian tombstones, and the sometimes unconsciously humorous epitaphs and inscriptions, make the Necropolis well worth a visit.

NOVELLES and NOVELETTES *[passim]*
Engineer MacPhail was the only member of the crew with any pretensions to literary taste: and his was restricted to the penny dreadfuls published weekly or fortnightly by the popular presses, the Edwardian equivalent of Mills and Boon though with fewer pretensions to creative merit. They were castigated and characterised by a contemporary commentator as being shortened novels distinguished only by triteness, triviality, sentimentality and a total lack of talent in execution.

QUARRIER'S HOMES *[I/20]*
The Victorian philanthropist William Quarrier founded his "Orphan Homes of Scotland" for abandoned or parentless children as what became virtually a self-contained village within the rural parish of Kilmacolm, Renfrewshire in 1876. By 1900, there were 1200 boys and girls in residence. Adjacent to these first homes, Quarrier later founded a Sanatorium for Consumptives and a Home for Epileptics.

RECHABITES *[I/5]*
One of the many serious, semi-serious and crank organisations devoted to the crusade for temperance in late Victorian and Edwardian Britain. The Rechabites took their creed from the stance of the abstinent sons of Rechab recounted in the book of Jeremiah. It is more than probable that much of their membership was just as backsliding as the mate of the **Vital Spark**, for the movement did not long survive as a force to be reckoned with.

SHEBEEN *[III/1]*

These were illegal drinking dens, unlicensed and usually doubly in defiance of the law in that much of the liquor they sold was itself the product of illicit stills. Often thought of as being unique to the remoter Highlands, such stills in fact were just about as common – at least in the time of Para Handy – in the cities themselves.

SINGERSES AT KILBOWIE [II/3]
At the turn of the century there would have been few homes in this country which did not proudly display, and use, their very own Singer Sewing Machine. The American manufacturers had established a huge factory at Clydebank on the north bank of the river, just inland from the great shipyards of John Brown and Yarrow, and for decades it was to employment for the women of its community what the yards were to employment for the men. The outstanding feature of the factory was its enormous clock-tower, rivalling Big Ben itself, which was a Clyde landmark for almost a century till the plant finally closed in the nineteen sixties. On the original Singer site there now stands the Clydebank Business Park: immediately behind it lies Kilbowie Stadium, home to Clydebank's professional football club.

SPAE-WIFE [II/12]
A female fortune teller, as popular at country fairs at the turn of the century as they are today: though nowadays the practitioner is as likely to style herself Gypsy Rose Lee as anything else.

SPALE BASKET [III/14]
A large, strong, shallow basket, the body made from broad lathes of wood. Ideal for Hurricane Jack's purpose of carrying as many empty bottles as possible.

TRUMP [I/17]
This was another name for the Jew's Harp, a tiny musical instrument of similar size – though very different sound –

to the harmonica. Basically a horseshoe-shaped metal frame with a central metallic tongue capable of vibrating when struck and capable of producing different notes when the instrument was gripped between the performer's front teeth.

Almost unheard of nowadays, it was a popular music-maker at the time of the **Vital Spark**: pocket-sized, portable, and quite surprisingly versatile in the hands of a capable performer. At an earlier date it was even played in the concert hall as a serious solo instrument.

WASHING-BOYNE *[I/9]*

A washing-boyne was a large, round wooden tub in which clothes were washed by hand. Given its shape and likely characteristics in a stormy sea, there could scarcely be a more appropriate analogy for the weatherly attributes of the **Vital Spark.**

CHAPTER 15

A Note on the Birlinn Edition

As a postscript, I would like to offer a few thoughts on the recent and well-produced omnibus volume of the Para Handy tales published under the Birlinn imprint. This, I believe, presents Para fans with an intriguing riddle but one which, at this late date, it is unlikely anyone will be able to answer with total assurance.

The three original collections of the stories were first published (months or even years after they had been featured in Neil Munro's columns in the *Glasgow Evening News*) in 1906, 1911 and 1923. In 1931, the year after the author's death, all three volumes were published together in omnibus form for the first time.

A debt is owed to the publisher and editors of this new Birlinn version of that edition, for the volume is much more than simply a reprint of what has gone before. It includes notes, comments and general background material: but most interestingly of all, it contains 18 "new" stories from the pages of the paper, copies of which are held on microfilm in Glasgow's Mitchell Library. None of these stories were included in the earlier, contemporary compilations and presumably (newspaper publishing being so ephemeral) they have been lying forgotten and unconsidered from the day after they appeared in print eighty years or so ago.

Of the new stories, the first (chronologically) was published on August 21, 1905, just seven months after the very first appearance of Para Handy in print in the edition of January 16: the second followed in November of the same year, and the third in January 1906. There is then a gap of more than six years before the fourth "uncollected" story was published in the paper in September 1912. The next 12 appeared at various dates throughout the war years, and the penultimate in August 1920. The last of all – *Wireless on the Vital Spark [BP/99]* – appeared in January 1924.

That was the year after the publication in book form of the third collection of the stories so, of course, that final story could not possibly have featured in it.

All the other seventeen, though, could have appeared in the book editions – yet none did. Why?

The editors of the Birlinn edition have suggested a reason for the exclusion of the war-time stories at least. Their thoughts are that this could have been due to the fact that Neil Munro "presumably chose to reduce the number of references to war-time events [which] must have seemed a little dated just a few years after the events."

I am not too sure about this. Many of the stories in the third published collection are very explicit war-time stories. The Mystery Ships: the enlistment and conscription process: war-time shortages: the peculiar and restrictive licensing laws of the time: these and other topics are the theme for many of the tales which appeared, as noted above, in the third compilation in 1923 and all twelve of the unpublished wartime stories were therefore candidates for inclusion in that collection.

My belief is that they were omitted from it – as the five pre-war stories had been also been ignored in compiling the collections – quite simply because most of them (possibly even all of them) were not written by Neil Munro himself, but were "ghosted" by another hand – or more likely hands.

Before trying to justify that claim I would emphasise that even if I am correct in that assumption this in no way detracts from the value of the additions which have been unearthed from long forgotten files and incorporated in the Birlinn edition. They are a part of the Para Handy repertoire whoever wrote them and if it was not Munro himself, then there is inevitably interest in speculating who might have penned them, and why.

Even on the very first reading, I was immediately convinced that there was something about these new stories that just did not feel quite "right". Every writer, and most especially any writer as gifted as Neil Munro, creates prose which has a distinct style and rhythm and structure. No two authors of note use identical cadences and fluencies of language: their use of words, their grammar and syntax, the rhythm and flow of their sentences, the construction of their plots and the delineation of their characters, are distinctly their own.

Nobody could mistake Stevenson for Scott, Kipling for Wells, or Hemingway for Huxley. Or, on a lighter note, P G Wodehouse's Bertie Wooster for Dornford Yates' Berry Pleydell.

I am convinced that the discrepancies of style which mark most of the new stories are so basic that they simply cannot be the work of Neil Munro – and that there are in addition creative and structural weaknesses and actual errors of fact in them which can only back up that proposition. Only by actually reading the stories can the validity (or otherwise) of my own grave doubts about their authenticity be properly judged, but one or two random examples of some of the more striking anomalies may help to clarify the thoughts behind the suggestion.

In *Para Handy's Shipwreck [BP 82]* Para, as narrator, indulges throughout in a preposterous hyperbole without parallel in any of the other tales. He is the smartest sailor on the Clyde, best swimmer in Scotland, strongest man in Britain, best jumper in the World: and the feats he accomplishes belong more in one of Hans Anderson's Fairy Tales. There is no credibility to the events narrated. They are farcical rather than whimsical and ludicrous rather than humorous.

Others of the new stories – such as *War-time on the Vital Spark [BP/86]: Thrift on the Vital Spark [BP/90]:* or *Sunny Jim Returns [BP 97]*, have tortuous or ill-defined story lines, where plainly-stated plot and logical dénouement are the staple ingredients of the collected tales.

In *The Vital Spark's Collision [BP/83]* the surnames of Dougie and of The Tar are given as Cameron and Dewar instead of Campbell and Turner. Neil Munro's continuity in the collected stories is so immaculate that it's hard to believe he could have made two errors such as this. Admittedly, at the time this story was published in the *News,* Dougie had not yet been given his Campbell surname: that is only established in *The Hair Lotion [II/13]* which appeared some time later. But I am sure that if Neil Munro had previously written a story in which Dougie was a Cameron, a Cameron he would have remained.

And as a final thought, it is almost as if the sub-editors on the *News* wanted to "flag" these stories to their readers in advance as being tales about the puffer and the exploits of her crew. Whereas in the 81 collected stories only 14 – that is to say just 17 per cent – have the names of either the skipper or the puffer in the title, no less than 10 – or 55 per cent – of just 18 "uncollected" stories do. A mere coincidence perhaps, but an odd one nevertheless.

Admittedly some of the new stories do sometimes exhibit at least a trace of the true Munro touch: for example *The Truth about the Push [BP/92]* has a very authentic story line, though that may be simple good fortune: and *Wireless on the Vital Spark, [BP/99],* which appeared too late to have been included in the last of the three collections, is in typical Munro vernacular.

* * * * *

Two questions remain to be asked if there is indeed any basis in fact for my speculation that these stories, or at least some of them, were by other hands. Why – and whose?

Why? Neil Munro was dismissive of the Para Handy stories, which he looked on as mere pot-boilers, a by-product of his journalistic career which impeded his serious writing activity. As the Birlinn editors themselves point out, he may have even have been trying to dispose of what he saw as a millstone round his neck (for much the same reasons as Conan Doyle tried to rid himself of Sherlock Holmes) when he married Para Handy off at the end of the first series. It was two years after the newspaper publication of that story before Para Handy appeared again in the columns of the *Glasgow Evening News* and in the interim Munro had only agreed to the publication of the first series in book form if they appeared under the authorial pseudonym of "Hugh Foulis".

The public wanted more and more of the **Vital Spark** but to its creator the puffer and her crew had apparently become simply an encumbrance and a literary embarrassment. Not hard to imagine that there would be times when he might have been content to allow someone else to satisfy the demand for "yet another" Para Handy story, particularly – and this is an important point – when they were always published anonymously in the paper, first as pieces on their own, but soon as a regular feature of the *Looker-On* column which he compiled, edited and largely wrote, but to which he never put his name.

By whom. My own feeling is that there are stylistic differences in the bulk of the new stories not just in comparison with the original collections but indeed when they are compared with each other. I see more than one hand involved and the simple answer would be that one or more of Munro's colleagues on the paper might have put together a story when column space demanded it, and the real progenitor of the **Vital Spark** was unwilling or unable to meet that demand.

* * * * *

There is, however, the intriguing possibility that

somebody who can actually be identified may have been the author of at least some of these new stories. For the facts on which this speculation can be based I am once again much indebted to Eoin McArthur, distant scion of the Munro family.

His paternal grandmother was a second cousin of Neil Munro and one of her daughters, Kate McArthur, Eoin's aunt, was born in 1876 and was brought up on Fyneside before marrying and moving to England. Kate had ambitions to write, and for advice, help and encouragement she in the 1890s contacted her already illustrious relative – working journalist and budding author Neil Munro.

The McArthur family still possess many of her letters to him, and his replies. He passes comments on the quality of work she has sent him for his opinion – sometimes favourably, sometimes critically. The letters show quite clearly that by the turn of the century he was accepting pieces and snippets from her for publication in the columns which he compiled for first the *Glasgow News* and, after its closure, the *Glasgow Evening News* – namely *The Lorgnette: Clydeside Echoes:* and *The Looker-On.*

This association continued after her marriage: in one letter written from her new home in England she states her intention of hopefully writing even more, in order to boost the family income.

Her brother, Eoin McArthur's father, told Eion half-a-century ago that Neil Munro at one stage had said that Kate could pen as good a newspaper paragraph as he did. And though there is no documentary evidence to back this up, it was always the family's understanding that she had actually written a few Para Handy tales – if only in the shape of a self-imposed "exercise" in improving her writing skills – and sent them to Neil Munro.

Did he use any of them? Since at no time were any of the published stories given a by-line in the paper there can be no proof of this, of course: but conversely the very absence of a by-line also means the possibility does exist. The actual authorship of the uncollected tales which appeared in the paper was not attributed. Therefore in theory, at least, they could have been written by anybody.

Certainly there has to be some reason why Munro excluded these 18 stories from the published collections: and some reason too for the fact that (in my view at least) the 18 stories in their chronological order do in general "improve" as they go on, with the very first, as suggested above, a rather naive attempt at the Para Handy style: and the very last a much closer relative of the real thing!

Read them: think about them: and decide for yourself.

We shall never know the facts at this late date and it is in any case a very minor literary puzzle. Like all puzzles, though, it is just that little touch tantalising and provides the sort of speculative embellishment to a tale of which Para himself would have approved.

EPILOGUE

The Last Puffer

There are still a few surviving puffers to be seen even today. The Scottish Maritime Museum at Irvine in Ayrshire includes the old **Spartan** in its collection of historic vessels and visitors can experience for themselves just how cramped and confined life on a working puffer must have been – and judge just how much at the mercy of the elements the little ships always were.

In and around the Caledonian and Crinan Canals and in the more sheltered waters of the western coasts two former **VIC** boats are still putting out to sea in the holiday season – though now with tourists as deck cargo. They come from all over the world to experience the unique ambiance of life afloat on boats which were really past their sell-by date even when they were launched, half a century ago. Motorists en route from Fort William to Inverness can thus suddenly be confronted by the unexpected sight of the **VIC** puffer **Auld Reekie** chugging down Loch Oich: visitors to the Crinan basin can watch the venerable **VIC 32** putting out to sea for a cruise among the Garvellach islands and on to Mull.

But in Ayr Harbour, at the mouth of the Clyde estuary, there is an even more astonishing sight. This once busy, now nearly deserted port is home base for the last – the very last – of the real working puffers.

Eilean Eisdeal is (inevitably!) a former **VIC**. She was built at Hull in 1944 and, at just 66 ft. overall, she was one of the smallest of the series and conforms exactly to the classic Scottish puffer size. Almost a century after the heyday of Para Handy, she is still providing an identical service to the most remote communities in Britain as that which was fulfilled by the **Vital Spark.**

She is operated by the splendidly-named Eisdale Island Shipping Line Ltd which has a tiny part-time office on Eisdale Island itself but which, effectively, is run from Warwick! The owner of the line, the boat, and the whole marvellously anachronistic concept is English shipping agent Chris Nicholson.

Chris has had a life-long love affair not just with the puffers but with the Western Highlands and Islands of Scotland. He was landlord of the real island of Eisdale when in 1983 he acquired the little puffer from her previous owner, Hugh Carmichael of Craignure in Mull.

For 10 years the last remaining lifeline bringing coal and other necessities to the distant islands and the scattered communities of the west has been run from an office in the heart of England, through a home port on the Ayrshire coast via a tiny infrequently-manned office on Eisdale Island.

Circumstances meant that Chris was forced to sell the island itself in 1988: but nothing would part him from the puffer which carries its Gaelic name.

Nothing. Despite the fact that running her is a labour of love rather than a sensible commercial commitment. He's spent about £200,000 on her already. Every year she has to undergo the most rigorous examination for her Board of Trade Certificate. Lose that, and she's finished. And then – what happens to the small island communities who rely solely and totally on **Eilean Eisdeal** for their winter's supply of coal?

There's nobody else to bring it in. The little three-handed puffer is their last hope. Chris provides a service which no commercial enterprise – one could almost say no rational individual! – would dream of providing. If a community needs a load of thirty or forty tons of coal then that can – just – be a job which will pay its way. But if two or three isolated houses at the end of a track from nowhere to nowhere need a puffer to beach with just a ton (or less) then economic madness sets in. That, though, is precisely the sort of service which the **Eilean Eisdeal** provides.

She goes to remote beaches with tiny cargos which the few remaining coasters could not reach and in any event, for sound commercial reasons, would not reach even if they could.

Chris is constantly lobbying the powers-that-be for just a tiny fraction of the financial largesse which is showered on the big, state-subsidised shipping services. As he says, if they need it then his own need has to be that much the greater: and if he goes out of business – what then for the communities to whom his little vessel has become a lifeline?

Eilean Eisdeal (unofficial motto: "We Go Anywhere") serves Barra and Eriskay: Coll and Tiree: Eigg, Rhum, Muck and Canna: Harris and Scalpay. There, and in many isolated bays on the west mainland, she often beaches to unload. Coal is her usual cargo. But she'll carry anything that's wanted and go any place where she's needed.

If there is any lingering doubt that the fighting spirit and the determination to suffer the slings and arrows of outrageous fortune which marked the crew of the **Vital Spark** ninety years ago are still alive in the crew of the **Eilean Eisdeal** today, consider this gem.

A year or two back, after having been delayed on passage from Ayr for several days by bad weather, she finally arrived in the Outer Isles and the harbour of Tarbert, Harris, with the community's winter supply of coal. On Christmas Eve.

"The folk came from miles around with cars and trucks and barrows and carts to get their shares," recalls Chris Nicholson. "When the boat was unloaded, the skipper got in touch with us to say he would leave straight away and try to get home in time for Boxing Day at best"

An hour out of Tarbert **Eilean Eisdeal** ran into a gale so fierce that there was no option but to return to harbour for shelter but having arrived, they couldn't get alongside the quay thanks to the direction of the wind and the force at which it was blowing. The puffer was forced to anchor in the bay.

They lay there for four days: and the only provisions aboard made even The Tar's catering on the **Vital Spark** seem like five star gourmet feasting. All they had after the first couple of days was a sack of potatoes, a couple of bottles of lemonade – and a packet of Bisto.

It's pleasing to be able to confirm that the last puffer, the last of her line, the last vestige of the world of Para Handy, got her crew back home in time to celebrate the New Year!

They deserved it!

The Stories

The Para Handy stories first appeared in the *Glasgow Evening News* over a period of about twenty years from the turn of the century. They were later published in a series of three volumes and then (for the first time in 1931) as an 'Omnibus' volume containing 81 published stories altogether, which was reprinted many times over the years. The first series appeared in book form with the title *The Vital Spark* and consists of 25 stories. Throughout this book they are identified by the Roman numeral I - to indicate the first collection - followed by an Arabic numeral (e.g. 24) to identify the individual story. The second series was published under the title *In Highland Harbours with Para Handy* and comprises 26 stories. They are identified here by the Roman numeral II followed by the appropriate Arabic numeral. The third series, *Hurricane Jack of the Vital Spark*, totalled 30 stories: the Arabic numeral identifying the individual tales is preceded by the Roman numeral III.

In 1991 Hugh Andrew's Birlinn Press brought out a brand new edition which included 18 stories, unearthed from the files of the old *Evening News*, which had never appeared in book form before, and which were appended to the 81 contained in the earlier editions. This brought the total number of tales in the Para Handy repertoire to 99. These newly published stories are identified by the prefix BP followed by the arabic numeral (82 to 99) assigned to them in the Birlinn edition. I am grateful to Hugh for allowing me to quote from, refer to and comment on the content of this valuable new addition to the bibliography of the Vital Spark.

223